The 2030 Caregiving Crisis

A Heavy Burden for Boomer Children

There won't be enough family caregivers for aging boomers.
It's time to add long-term personal care to Medicare
and start training the millions of aides
we'll need to help out.

Henry Moss

TABLE OF CONTENTS

Acknowledgments

I'd like to thank the public service organizations that have advocated tirelessly for older adults, family caregivers, and the personal care aides, home health aides, and certified nurse aides who are the real heroes of this story. AARP, PHI, FCA, Consumer Voice, SEIU, ASA, the Alzheimer's Association, and many others have pulled together the research and analysis that makes a book like this possible.

My family and friends have been incredibly supportive of the effort despite their wish that I had taken on a less depressing topic. Gilbert and Fran reviewed early drafts and Fran managed the technical production process. I would especially like to thank Rikka for her detailed proofreading and excellent editorial suggestions.

I would also like to thank Maizlyn ("Pam") who took such great care of my mother when she became an "oldest old" and needed round-the-clock care. We will need many more like her. Hence this book.

Preface

My mother typically dozed off early and was wide awake at 4 a.m. or earlier. Parkinson's and congestive heart failure had made her exceedingly frail, and she was exhibiting signs of dementia. The Medicaid-authorized aide did not arrive at my mother's tiny apartment in the senior facility until 9 a.m. for her eight-hour stint, the maximum available.

I got the Medi-alert agency calls in the wee hours, and my wife and I stayed with her at the ER for as many as 18 hours. There were five falls that year, yielding one hip replacement and three 30-day rehab stays in a nursing home.

Intense anxiety and tedium accompanied the hours my wife and I spent waiting in the ER or at my mother's home, giving me a glimpse of how such caregiving might lead to depression. I was trapped in a role I didn't want. My mother didn't want me in the role either, and kept telling me to go home. The nursing home rehab stays were intolerable for her. She would sit in her wheelchair in the hall near the nurse's station for hours, despite serious back pain. My wife and I felt the need to visit daily and advocate for her needs.

Most approaches to preventing or ameliorating caregiver burden are reactive. They take the family caregiver role as a given and suggest moderating burden through adult daycare, respite services, counseling, and social support networks. While certainly useful, these approaches have only a limited impact and will certainly not be available to the extent needed over the next three decades.

A proactive approach would aim to diminish the family caregiver role. This is where personal care aides come in, particularly those deployed round-the-clock in the client's home. In addition to dealing with the usual activities of daily living, they prevent falls, manage sleep-cycle problems, assure medication compliance, and handle tasks set by visiting nurses. They also prepare favored foods, tune in favored TV shows, get clients out for fresh air, and prepare for family visitors. A personal care aide can be far more attentive than can an overworked nurse aide in a nursing home. They can also respond quickly to client discomfort or need, avoiding the frustrating and depressing wait times typical of nursing homes.

There are many issues to be addressed in expanding the use of round-the-clock in-home aides, especially the turnover associated with the job's poor pay and training. Better compensation and meaningful benefits will reduce turnover and attract more workers to the field. Aides must become valued paraprofessionals and an important part of case management.

My mother's geriatrician filled out forms indicating she needed a 24-hour personal care aide to help with activities of daily living. The New York City Medicaid program is one of the most generous in the nation and authorizes 24-hour care if the client is medically stable and he or she (or a nearby family member or friend) is able to direct care. New York wants to keep older adults out of nursing homes, believing it best for the client and expecting it to be cost-effective in the long run.

The agency aides we saw were poorly paid, minimally trained, and sometimes semi-literate, but we were lucky to eventually get a wonderful woman who worked five days a week (a second aide came for the other two) for years. She understood the idiosyncratic needs of a cranky, incontinent, and increasingly demented elder. My mother lived out her life comfortably, in her apartment. My wife and I managed her affairs and visited regularly. We were deeply relieved.

Introduction

The United States lacks a long-term care system. The closest it has is Medicaid, a safety net program for the very poor. According to the U.S. Department of Health and Human Services, at least 90% of older persons receiving help with activities of daily living (ADLs) in 2011 relied on some "informal" care, from family members and friends. About two thirds relied on only informal care. Family and friends collectively provided 75–80% of total care hours in non-institutional settings (Spillman, Wolff, Freedman, & Kasper, 2014). Help with ADLs involves one or more basic daily functions, including dressing, self-feeding, grooming, toileting, bathing, transferring (e.g., into and out of bed) and moving from one place to another.

Keeping an older adult in the community using round-the-clock formal care is an expensive proposition. Community Medicaid will pay for some custodial care at home, but rarely beyond six hours daily. With most states in budget crisis, even limited services are difficult to access and long waiting lists are common. When paying privately for care is unaffordable, family members assume the burden by default. Older adults without available family help are consigned to nursing facilities or risk health and safety by remaining alone in their homes.

Most family caregivers today are motivated by an intense desire to keep loved ones out of the understaffed and under-resourced nursing homes they see as little more than warehouses for disabled and demented older adults waiting to die. Even when they can afford elite nursing facilities, family members still face the emotional distress that inevitably accompanies this late-life transition. It is not surprising that the number of people residing long-term in nursing homes has dropped over recent decades, even as the number of older adults needing care at this level has remained the same (Redfoot & Houser, 2010).

The situation is about to get worse. The tidal wave of baby boomer retirement is upon us along with the "birth dearth" that followed. Family caregivers, adult children in particular, face bleak prospects. Adult children of boomers, Generation X and early Millennials, will be dealing with work obligations, their children's college expenses, the effects of the recent recession, and ongoing economic stagnation. They will be hard-pressed to take on the extent of caregiving that will be needed by the huge boomer generation.

This book makes the case for recruiting and training millions of additional personal care aides as boomers age into their 80s and face chronic illness and severe disability. The aides will be needed to assure safety and emotional well-being and to relieve overburdened family members. They should be deployed into private homes, senior residences, and even nursing homes to ensure quality person-centered care for up to 24/7. Medicare, or a new insurance program, should make such assistance universally available.

The 2030 problem

We are well aware that the retirement and aging of baby boomers over the 40-year period from 2010 to 2050 will present problems to advanced nations, including the United States. Some call it the Silver Tsunami. Demographers, epidemiologists, economists, and sociologists have been digging into the numbers and a large literature has emerged describing the many potentially serious social and economic problems that are likely to accompany a rapidly aging population. The scale and pace of aging is unprecedented for modern advanced societies and is already reaching into developing nations, notably China.

This book argues that most of the analyses and predictions used in policy discussions in the U.S. underestimate the extent and depth of what we will be facing. In particular, they do not appreciate the implications of what some refer to as the "2030 problem". 2030 is when retired boomers start becoming octogenarians in large numbers. Between 2030 and 2050 the size of this "oldest old" population will explode, increasing 3.5 times compared to its size in 2010, becoming by far the fastest-growing segment of the population. The age 80+ population in the United States will grow from 11 million in 2010 to 18 million in 2030, and 35 million in 2050, while the overall population increases only marginally (Redfoot, Feinberg, & Houser, 2013).

Who will care for the oldest old boomers? The birth dearth that followed the postwar boom has created an acute problem. In 2010 there were 7.2 available family caregivers 45–64 years of age for every American 80 years of age and older. According to the Public Policy Institute at the American Association for Retired Persons (AARP), using census-based projections, by 2050 there will be only 2.9 family caregivers for this population, a drop of over 50% (Redfoot et al., 2013). As the number of oldest old accelerates upward, the number of available family caregivers accelerates downward (Figures 1 and 2). Husbands, wives, sisters, and brothers will have increasingly limited roles as caregivers as they, too, reach very old age. It will be the small cohort of middle-aged children of boomers facing this caregiving nightmare in 2030-2050.

Figure 1. Caregiver support ratio, U.S.

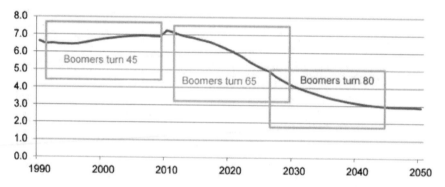

Source: AARP report "The Aging of the Baby Boom and the Growing Care Gap: A Look at Future Declines in the Availability of Family Caregivers," by Donald Redfoot, Lynn Feinberg, and Ari Houser. Calculations are based on REMI (Regional Economic Models, Inc.) 2013 baseline demographic projections. Reproduced with permission from the AARP Public Policy Institute.

Note: The caregiver support ratio is the ratio of the population aged 45–64 to the population aged 80-plus.

Figure 2. Projected age 54–65 population, U.S. (in millions)

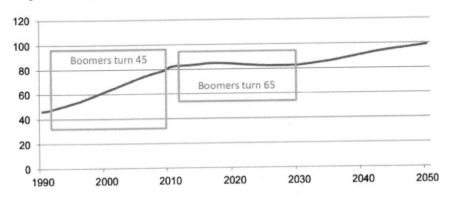

Source: : AARP report "The Aging of the Baby Boom and the Growing Care Gap: A Look at Future Declines in the Availability of Family Caregivers," by Donald Redfoot, Lynn Feinberg, and Ari Houser. Calculations are based on REMI (Regional Economic Models, Inc.) 2013 baseline demographic projections. Reproduced with permission from the AARP Public Policy Institute.

Will the 2030 caregiver problem become a crisis?

Most analysts and policymakers agree that an aging society creates problems. Many focus on potential labor shortages and the pressure placed on social security systems. Social Security and Medicare are expected to develop solvency problems that suggest, to some, a need for sacrifice in the form of retirement age increases, reduced benefits, and increased payroll taxes on younger workers.

Most believe that such problems, while troublesome, will be tractable. Boomers, they say, are healthier and wealthier than prior cohorts. With fewer boomers doing manual labor, they will work into their 70s, be healthier in their 80s, and suffer only a small window of disability before death. Such a "compression of disability" will mean that fewer caregivers will be needed, relatively speaking. Retiring later will help prevent labor shortages, they say, and a slow growth economy could have salutary effects by mitigating resource depletion, global warming, and uncontrolled immigration. After 2050, demographics will rebalance and we will be in a position to focus on quality instead of quantity of growth. While an aging society is not ideal, they say, there is no need to panic.

A major crisis

This optimistic assessment ignores some important factors that will move front and center by 2030 and turn a problem into a crisis. The first is the sheer magnitude of the problem. Compression of disability is at best a questionable assumption and if the extension of lifespans is occurring mainly through management of chronic conditions, this may only prolong the period of disability, dementia, and frailty for many of the oldest old. Any compression effect will be dwarfed by the sheer scale of the overall problem.

The second factor is the lack of long-term care insurance and a less-than-anticipated savings cushion for boomer retirees. The third is the inadequacy of institutional and community Medicaid.

A fourth and often-ignored factor is the reality of the caregiving process, its intensity, and its effect on family caregivers. Middle-aged children of boomers, many of whom will be "sandwiched" between managing their children and their parents, face a caregiving burden potentially much greater than that being assumed by current family caregivers. The emotional, physical, and financial strain will be overwhelming to many.

The seriousness of this last factor is best captured by considering the caregiving needs of those with dementia, the most stressful and demanding type of custodial care. According to the Alzheimer's Association (2014a), about 15 million family members and friends provided 17.7 billion hours of unpaid care to those with Alzheimer's disease and other dementias in 2013, over 1,000 hours of care per caregiver. With dementia prevalence expected to triple by 2050 (Hebert, Weuve, Scherr, & Evans, 2013), this could rise to over 50 billion hours.

The dementia problem goes to the heart of the impending crisis. Older adults in the more advanced stages of dementia cannot be safely left alone, yet they often have behavioral problems that challenge even the most patient caregiver. Who will care for these elders? Will boomer children be forced to leave the workforce in large numbers? How many boomers will live alone with dementia or severe disability, or be warehoused in under-resourced nursing homes?

The moral imperative of caregiving

As in many other societies, there is an expectation in the U.S. that, regardless of what the government may or may not contribute, it is up to children to care for their parents and other family members when they are unable to care for themselves. Most will institutionalize a parent only under the direst circumstances. Even then, they will suffer continuing psychological stress sensing the depression, anxiety, and anger their loved ones feel upon entry into even the best of nursing homes.

The moral quality of this expectation keeps family caregivers from complaining and leads them to take on extraordinary burdens. The suffering is in silence. The silence, unfortunately, keeps long-term care out of the public spotlight and low on the policy agenda.

Chapter One describes the scale of the impending 2030 caregiving problem in more detail. It discusses specific characteristics of the boomer generation, including divorce rates, childlessness, and retirement finances. It also examines characteristics of boomer children, including their economic and family circumstances. It finds that the capacity of these children to contribute to the care of their parents will be limited.

Chapter Two discusses boomer health, especially risk factors for disability. It considers positive trends that appear to be leading to a compression of disability. It also considers the worrisome possibility that, due largely to the effects of obesity, stress, and associated metabolic and neurological disorders, levels of care need for boomers when they become the oldest old may, in fact, be worse than anticipated. Of particular concern is the possibility that those disabilities requiring the most intensive caregiving, namely dementia, mobility impairment, and frailty syndrome, will become more prevalent than projected. Dementia, in particular, will be the source of the greatest caregiving concern.

Chapter Three examines family caregiver burden, focusing on its psychological and emotional impact. Family caregiving is, in itself, a burdensome enterprise with significant economic and social effects. Dementia, and the presence of especially negative mood, anxiety, or agitation in an older family member can amplify caregiver distress, impacting the psychological and physical well-being of the caregiver.

Chapter Four discusses the capacity of the nursing home industry in the U.S. to deal with the impending crisis. Real and perceived problems have created a poor public image for these institutions, creating an intense aversion to nursing home placement. This, in turn, has led to a redirecting of public funds away from nursing homes, further worsening their lot, and toward the recent movement for de-institutionalization and "culture change". Nursing homes will clearly have to play a part in a world experiencing a rapidly declining family caregiver population, especially for those suffering from dementia and other conditions requiring round-the-clock care. Can we deal effectively with their shortcomings?

Chapter Five looks at innovations and reforms either underway or proposed for the nursing home sector. Dementia "special care units" show promise for providing the kind of care required for those with moderate to advanced Alzheimer's disease and other dementias. The "Green House" model, promoting small nursing homes that provide person-centered care in home-like environments, has shown some success in overcoming the sterile, medicalized environment of traditional nursing homes, and increasing resident satisfaction. Similar culture change has also been proposed for the larger nursing homes that serve poor, severely disabled, Medicaid-dependent populations. Even promising reforms struggle with cost factors, however, and currently serve mostly the more affluent. Changing the culture of traditional homes will require confronting significant resource shortfalls, especially in direct care worker staffing.

Chapter Six considers "assisted living" and its potential to mitigate the 2030 crisis. The demand for long-term care services in the community has led to the emergence of a large, for-profit assisted living industry. In the current system, however, services are aimed primarily at those who can afford to pay privately. Efforts to include middle- and low-income residents are underway but face formidable challenges.

Chapter Seven continues the discussion of alternatives to nursing homes and considers formal in-home care. As with assisted living, this kind of care is too expensive on a private pay basis. Since it is still less expensive than assisted living and nursing homes, however, and is clearly the preferred option for older adults and their families, there is considerable interest in finding ways to fund new programs that allow older adults to "age in place" in their homes and communities. These programs, including the successful Program for All-Inclusive Care for the Elderly, or PACE, face a number of obstacles and are already feeling the effect of state and federal efforts to hold down costs.

Chapter Eight focuses on policy solutions and concludes that only a federally-financed universal long-term personal care insurance program can make a serious dent in the problem. This would be, in effect, adding personal care services to Medicare. Millions of personal care workers could then be deployed to provide up to round-the-clock custodial and basic medical care to disabled older adults, in their homes, in assisted living facilities, and in nursing homes.

Such workers are expected to be in short supply over the next decades. They will need to be compensated at higher rates and have better working conditions and training. Personal care aides must become respected paraprofessionals.

Medicare became a reality 50 years ago when the vast majority of citizens, across the political spectrum and all social classes, saw that improving the health of the older population would benefit society at large. Adding long-term personal care to that benefit is long overdue and essential to addressing the 2030 crisis.

Chapter One

Characteristics of retiring boomers and their children

There were 11 million people age 80 years and older in the U.S. in 2010. In 2030 there will be nearly 20 million and by 2050 there will be 33 million. The sheer size of the post-war boomer cohort relative to the cohort immediately following will make the 80+ age group the fastest-growing segment of the population by far in 2030–2050 (Redfoot et al., 2013). The 2030 crisis will be driven by the needs of this growing cohort of oldest old in the face of the declining numbers of available family caregivers, adult children in particular. It will reach its peak over the course of the two decades from 2030 to 2050.

The next chapter will address the likely extent of boomer disability and caregiving need in 2030–2050. This chapter examines the scope and scale of the impending family caregiver shortfall, and socioeconomic characteristics of boomers and their adult children that will contribute to the problem.

Keeping older adults out of nursing homes

After age 80, the prospect of institutionalization becomes a major concern. Yet, nursing homes are anathema to aging boomers and family members indicate a strong desire to keep aging relatives out of the nursing home system for as long as possible. This desire is driven, in part, by quality of care issues. It is also driven by the growth of private home ownership over the last 50 years and changing societal norms. According to AARP, citing the National Long-term Care Survey, institutional use declined by 37% between 1984 and 2004 and the number of people living in the community with need for assistance with two or more activities of daily living (ADLs) rose by two thirds (Redfoot & Houser, 2010).

AARP also reported that 68% of Americans believe they will be able to rely on their families when they require help (Redfoot et al., 2013) and a Pew survey indicated that most adult children of boomers (86% of Millennials and 78% of Generation X) expect to be taking care of a parent or other older adult in their lifetime. The same survey showed that, despite popular beliefs about the so-called self-centered character of boomer children, early Millennials and Generation X place a higher value on caring for parents than did prior generations (Pew Research Center, 2011). The trend is perhaps influenced by immigrant families, including those in the fast-growing Asian and Latino communities, where taking care of older family members is a strong cultural norm (AARP, 2014; Pharr, Francis, Terry, & Clark, 2014).

Another Pew survey report found that the U.S. had the second-lowest level of belief that government should be financially responsible for care among 21 countries surveyed. The older adult and her family are expected to carry the burden of financial responsibility (Pew Research Center, 2014).

Resistance to placing older adults in nursing homes has actually worsened the quality of care in these facilities. State and federal budgeting for long-term care has recently tilted toward community-based care, further limiting resources for nursing home improvements. Several other factors are adding to the "squeeze" on nursing homes, as reported by Kaiser Health News (Yoder, 2012):

- Many of the homes built in the 1960s are not suited to modern care and have been shuttered.
- Private financing for new private nursing home construction dropped during the recent recession. Between 2007 and 2011, new units under construction declined by one third.
- Medicaid and Medicare reimbursement levels for nursing home care have declined, with total Medicaid losses in 2011 of $6.3 billion nationally. Medicare reimbursements for short-term rehabilitation stays, which constituted 20% of nursing home revenue, dropped by 11%.
- The real estate collapse in 2007 wiped out trillions in home equity, reducing the ability of individuals to use home equity to fund nursing home residency.

Financial pressure on nursing homes has meant that standards for nursing home staffing levels are not being met, and that safety and quality of care issues in nursing homes remain largely unaddressed (Long Term Care Community Coalition, 2013).

Nursing homes should be receiving significant added funding for improvement given a rapidly aging population. Yet, the politics of the situation makes this unlikely. Conservatives emphasize self-reliance and want to curb the growth of government-funded social assistance programs. Liberals and progressives are caught up in the community care movement and its promise of a humane approach to caring for the oldest old. Nursing homes receive inadequate attention, which will place added pressure on the families of older adults who may need institutionalization.

Boomer finances: Can they contribute to their own care?

Boomers are thought to constitute the wealthiest generation ever, and, in a technical sense, they are wealthier as a group. But when looked at from the standpoint of individuals needing long-term care, the situation is not nearly so bright.

"Mean" vs. "median" wealth

Many boomers are very wealthy and contribute disproportionately to the establishment of a mean, or average, wealth for the cohort. Due to the rise of wealth inequality, however, the mean is not the best way to characterize the wealth of boomers. In fact, when looked at in terms of numbers of individuals in different quartiles, *median* wealth, the situation shifts significantly. Even pre-recession numbers are ominous. For example, data from a 2004 Federal Health and Retirement Study (HRS) of a group of "early" boomers born between 1948 and 1953 showed that at 51 to 56 years of age their mean total net worth (roughly, investment wealth + home equity) was $390,000 in 2004 dollars (Lusardi & Mitchell, 2006). The median total net worth, however, was only $152,000, 2.5 times less. This is a substantial skewing of the wealth picture. Even more concerning, the lowest two quartiles of middle-aged boomers were financially weaker than expected. The bottom quartile showed an average of only $36,000 in total net worth in 2004 (Lusardi & Mitchell, 2006).

Excluding housing wealth, since it is not readily available to meet day-to-day expenses, the median available wealth for the lowest two quartiles dropped even further, to $47,500 and $7,000, respectively. Indeed, the bottom 10% had negative available wealth, i.e., net indebtedness (Lusardi & Mitchell, 2006).

If this pattern holds for younger boomers, already facing stagnant incomes and underemployment, a large and unexpected number of pre-retirees will be approaching retirement in poor shape. The lowest two quartiles of all boomers, 35 million strong, will have difficulty meeting normal retirement expenses. The bottom quartile, many with poverty-level incomes, could face significant deprivation.

The same HRS study showed that the lowest quartile of the prior generation, those who were 51 to 56 years of age in 1992, actually had higher net worth than the 2004 study group (Lusardi & Mitchell, 2006). Although home equity wealth was slightly lower, that generation was more likely to have a defined benefit plan, i.e., a pension, to supplement social security.

The reasons for the weak retirement financial situation of the lowest two quartiles of boomers are many:

- The decline of defined benefit pensions left workers with low incomes only the "choice" to contribute to a 401K or IRA. Participation levels, as expected, have been poor, particularly during the crucial early years of employment. The tax benefits of making contributions were supposed to motivate savings, but the benefit for those lowest on the income scale were just too small to be meaningful.
- Education expenses rose dramatically for boomers as they sought higher education for themselves and their children. According to the

National Center for Policy Analysis, education expenditures rose 80% for those 45 to 54 years of age between 1990 and 2010 (Villareal, 2012).

- Healthcare expenses also rose between 1990 and 2010, by 30% for those 45 to 54 years of age and 21% for those 55 to 64 years of age. Housing-related expenses grew as well, by 25% for both groups over this same span (Villareal, 2012).

- While expenses rose over the 30-year period for middle- and lower-income boomers, incomes remained basically flat, leaving little surplus to invest. The decline of unions contributed to the wage effect, leaving many to fend for themselves in the labor market, placing further pressure on wages and higher risk for unemployment and underemployment (Mishel, Gould, & Bivens, 2015).

- A greater part of wealth has been tied up in home value for boomers than for previous generations. The majority of even low-income boomers own their own homes. While this counts as wealth, it is less liquid than other sources and limits the ability to meet day-to-day expenses (Lusardi & Mitchell, 2006).

- Boomers grew up in the suburbs that arose after World War II. Suburban life created an entire new layer of lifestyle expense that did not exist in urban centers. Cars became ubiquitous and even two cars were considered a necessity if there were several family members who needed to commute to work or school. Between 1960 and 2000, the number of households with two or more cars nearly tripled (Table 1). Children were expected to go to college and their academic and social standing in high school was important to parents. Credit card debt, which barely existed after the war, skyrocketed as families took advantage of new technologies that have become standard in homes, from dishwashers to color TVs. As the number of two-worker households grew, expenditures on prepared foods and labor-saving technologies, like microwaves, dryers, and self-defrosting refrigerators, grew rapidly.

Table 1. Cars per household (percentage), U.S., 1960–2000

Year	No cars	One car	Two or more cars
1960	21.53%	56.94%	21.53%
1970	17.47%	47.71%	34.83%
1980	12.92%	35.53%	51.54%
1990	11.53%	33.74%	54.68%
2000	9.35%	33.79%	56.86%

Source: U.S. Census

Impact of the recession

The recession of 2008 and beyond took a significant bite out of the wealth of retiring boomers, including home equity and retirement investments. While much of that loss has been recovered since 2010, this means that boomer wealth did not grow in absolute terms for years. It also means that boomers who had shifted their wealth into more conservative, low-risk investments as they approached retirement have been less able to take advantage of recovering equity markets.

Although markets are recovering and the economy is slowly improving, the employment situation, especially for younger boomers, is problematic. Losing a job at 50 years of age can be devastating. Transitioning to a new job is fraught with difficulty. Such workers can be victimized by narrow or outdated skill sets or prior income levels that cannot or will not be met by new employers who rightly expect such new employees to "keep looking" if hired. Boomers who lose jobs also face geographical challenges and the threat of bankruptcy, foreclosure, and bad credit ratings.

The result has been significant growth in underemployment, that is, middle-aged boomers working temporary, part time, or full time at lower wages than in their previous job. A 2012 AARP survey report showed that 56% of unemployed, then re-employed, boomers who preferred full-time work were only working part-time, double the number of those continuously employed in the same job (AARP, 2012). Underemployment makes it even harder to add to retirement savings and such employment usually comes with few or no benefits.

At the same time, debt, associated with education loans, mortgage and home equity loans, credit cards, and medical expenses, has pushed many boomers into crisis management over recent years. Data from the Administrative Office of the U.S. Courts show that in 2007 nearly half of all individuals (42%) filing for bankruptcy in the United States were boomers between the ages of 45 and 64. They also show that the number of bankruptcy filings of individuals between 55 and 64 years of age increased by 65% during the five-year period of 2002-2007 while filings by individuals 25 years of age and younger decreased by 60% during the same period (Morath, 2010). Bankruptcies increased further during the recession and half of boomers surveyed by AARP reported serious financial hardship (AARP, 2012)

Foreclosures have also risen for boomers. A 2012 AARP survey report showed a marked increase in delinquent mortgages and foreclosures for those between 50 and 64 years of age in 2011. It also reported the foreclosure rate for this group rising by a factor of ten between 2007 (.31%) and 2011 (2.98%), representing hundreds of thousands of homeowners (Trawinski, 2012).

In sum, while boomer wealth is technically greater than the wealth of prior generations and will help make lives somewhat easier in the early stages of retirement, the reality facing millions of boomers is that this wealth may not be enough to cover their needs when they become the oldest old. According to a 2014 AARP report, only 10% of those 50 years of age and older had purchased long-term care insurance. While there are a number of reasons why insurance is not acquired, cost is the major reason given (Reinhard et al., 2014).

Childless boomers and divorced boomers

Boomers did not have many children and this will be the main source of the 2030 caregiving problem. There are aspects of boomer family structure, however, that may amplify the problem in the late stages of life.

Childlessness

Children are not spread evenly across the boomer population. According to AARP, there are currently 15 million childless baby boomers and, by 2040, childless boomers will make up 21% of the oldest old. In 2010, one in nine women 80 to 84 years of age had no children. By 2030, they project that one in six will be childless. By 2050, one in five at that age will be childless, nearly doubling the 2010 number (Redfoot et al., 2013). The percentage of adults 45 to 54 years of age who have never married tripled between 1986 and 2009. (Redfoot et al., 2013).

While the lifespan gap between men and women has narrowed over recent decades, its promise of more intact marriages in old age has been counterbalanced by a significant increase in boomer divorce after age 50 (Brown & Lin, 2012). This further ensures that more people than ever will be living alone in their 80s and 90s. These numbers are worrisome. Those without both spouses and adult children will find themselves with severely limited care options.

Childless single women in their 80s will be especially vulnerable as they will likely be more in need of intensive caregiving. According to the Alzheimer's Association (2014), they are diagnosed with Alzheimer's at twice the rate of men, and the Centers for Disease Control and Prevention (CDC) estimates that women at 80 years of age suffer arthritis at rates 39% higher than men at that age (Theis, Helmick, & Hootman, 2007). Other studies have shown that older women suffer from "frailty syndrome", characterized by muscle wasting, loss of weight, fatigue, and disability, at nearly twice the rate of men (Clegg, Young, Iliffe, Rikkert, & Rockwood, 2013). As will be discussed in Chapter Two, these conditions are major drivers of the need for intensive daily caregiving.

Older single boomer women will also be less financially secure, on average, and less able to pay privately for assistance or join an assisted living community. Lower social security rates, due to years spent out of the workplace, and limited savings, mean that such women will be faced with institutionalization in large numbers (Torres, 2014).

Nieces and nephews of older childless women may feel pressure to help, even as they are faced with caring for their own aging parents.

Divorced boomers and living alone

The divorce rate in couples over 50 years of age has more than doubled over the last 20 years. In 1990, less than one in 10 divorcees was 50 years of age or older. In 2009, that figure was one in four (Brown & Lin, 2012).

Many older divorcees live alone. In 1950, only 10% of all Americans over 65 years of age lived alone. Today, one third live alone, a figure that rises to 40% for those 85 years of age and older (Klinenberg, Torres, & Portacolone, 2013). A 2013 New York University study showed that many older adults living alone, including widowers, prefer to live that way, reflecting a desire to remain in their own homes and not be a burden on children (Klinenberg et al., 2013)

It is unclear what impact this trend will have on the caregiving situation as boomers become the oldest old, but it raises several concerns. The first relates to the geographical proximity of family members. Children with intact two-parent marriages are better able to manage caregiving due to potentially available support by a spouse and the need to deal with only a single location. Significant obstacles arise when a divorce causes parents to live a long distance from each other and caregivers may have to split their time.

A second concern involves the willingness of adult children to provide support for parents who have undergone divorce. A 2008 survey found that children of divorced parents were less inclined to provide financial or caregiving support, all else being equal (Pezzin, Pollock, & Schone, 2008).

A third concern arises in cases of divorce with remarriage. Stepparents are often a source of tension when it comes to caregiving. Stepchildren are generally less willing to provide support to step-parents. Some may feel particularly burdened if forced to provide care for a step-parent whose biological family members are unwilling to help. A step-child, or any adult child, may even be faced with caring for two parents and two step-parents (Pezzin et al., 2008).

A fourth concern is the trend of boomers away from traditional community networks that have historically provided support for the disabled. They are less likely than prior generations to participate in local religious, civic, and charitable organizations, for example, and less likely to ask for community assistance generally (Harvard School of Public Health–MetLife Foundation, 2004).

A final and underappreciated concern relates to the contingent circumstances that inevitably arise in the course of aging. Adults over 80 years of age living alone, divorced, or otherwise, face the unpredictability of transitions. This will be discussed further in later chapters, but circumstances surrounding the care situation can be unforgiving. One day an older adult seems fine. Then there is a fall, hospitalization, possibly surgery, and 30 days in a rehabilitation facility. This stressful series of events can drain the energy and spirit of a very old parent leading to rapid deterioration caused by poor sleep, loss of appetite, anxiety, and depression. This in turn causes further loss of mobility and further mental decline in a vicious cycle leading to increased frailty and helplessness.

Within a matter of weeks or months, such situations can require significant action by an adult child who may be ill-prepared for such a profound, but all-too-common, transformation. Older adults and their families rarely plan for such contingencies yet they can be life-altering for all involved. While children may want their parents to live in their own homes for as long as possible, even when alone, circumstances can make it difficult to prepare for and respond to the realities of aging.

Adult children of boomers

Generation X and older Millennials will have a substantial role to play in the long-term care of their boomer parents, uncles, and aunts. The numbers are unforgiving, as we have shown. Contrary to popular characterizations, a very large number within these generations expect to play a role in the care of their boomer parents and relatives, and see it as a moral responsibility. However, many boomer children may lack the the capacity to provide sufficient care and support.

Financial capacity

Generation X lived through three financial calamities in the U.S. The first involved the bursting of the "dotcom" bubble in the 1990s. Though they were young at the time, this created a meaningful delay in investment earnings for those involved in the market. The second was the housing market collapse that commenced in 2007. The problem in this case was that many Generation X families purchased homes at the peak of the housing market and suffered correspondingly large losses in the downturn. According to a Pew study, GenXers lost 27% of their home equity in the collapse, compared to only 14% for early boomers. Many suffered foreclosures, or switched to renting, and have not been able to take full advantage of the recent rebound in housing values (Pew Charitable Trust, 2013).

The third calamity was the recession that commenced in 2008. According to a 2014 Pew Charitable Trust report, Generation X as a group lost nearly half its wealth between 2007 and 2010, a larger decline than that of any other generation. Only one third of this cohort had more wealth than their parents had at the same age and this despite the fact that 75%

of GenXers have higher incomes, controlling for family size and inflation, than their parents had (Pew Charitable Trust, 2014).

The financial calamities and loss of asset wealth have created a so-called "education paradox". GenXers and Millennials are more highly educated than boomers. More have college degrees and many more have graduate and professional degrees. Fifty-four percent of boomers had only a HS diploma or less when they were 25 to 32 years of age while only 46% of Generation X and just 37% of Millennials had only a high school degree or less in that age range (Pew Charitable Trust, 2014). While higher education levels account for the higher incomes of this generation, on average, the past strong association of education levels with asset wealth has not held for boomer children.

Compounding the wealth problem is indebtedness. In 2011, GenXers who carried debt carried six times more debt than their parents did at the same age (Pew Charitable Trust, 2014). The dramatic growth of indebtedness has many sources, but the largest, by far, involves student loan debt, a major reason for the education "paradox" (Table 2). Over 50% of the current $1 trillion dollars in student loan debt is held by Generation X, with Millennials holding 40% (Pew Charitable Trust, 2014).

This weak financial outlook has made GenXers pessimistic about their own retirement prospects, especially given the likelihood that they will live longer, on average, than their parents (Pew Research Center, 2014). This constrains their ability to help their parents, financially and otherwise.

The future of the bottom quartile of boomer children appears particularly bleak. The boomer generation is largely white (over 70%) and non-immigrant. The Gen X and Millennial generations are more diverse, with only 56–58% white and more minorities and immigrants, including many with limited language skills (Pew Research Center, 2015). While income inequality has had its effect on the distribution of income and wealth, as it did for boomers, the bottom quartile, containing a high percentage of low-income immigrants and less advantaged minorities, will be especially likely to be poor. Many in this poorest group are also saddled with student loan debt on top of everything else (Huelsman, 2015), and have negative net worth. Yet they will still have to deal with aging parents, some of whom will be overseas.

Table 2. Average total student loan debt for baccalaureate degree recipients who borrowed, 1994–2009.

Average cumulative amount borrowed for undergraduate education					
In dollars at the time			In 2009 dollars		
1994	2001	2009	1994	2001	2009
$10,100	$18,000	$24,700	$14,700	$21,800	$24,700

Source: Adapted from the 2012 Web Tables (NCES 2013-156) of the National Center for Education Statistics, U.S. Department of Education.

The impact of financial stress

The bleak financial circumstances facing boomer children has affected, or will affect, other aspects of their lives:

- Adult children of boomers have married later, or not all, and are having children later. Forty-eight percent of boomers were married by age 32. Only 36% of GenXers were married by that age and 26% of Millennials (Pew Research Center, 2015). This increases the likelihood that they will be "sandwiched" between taking care of their parents and their children.

- Many adult children of boomers have decided against having children, including 42% of college-educated millennial women, due, primarily, to financial stress (Alcorn, 2014). While commitment to pursuing a career contributes to the decision not to have children, the ability to balance work and child-raising can be compromised by debt and a poor financial outlook. The decision not to have children is often made reluctantly.

- GenXers will need to stay in the labor force longer to make up for retirement savings shortfalls. Of particular concern are the employment levels projected for middle-aged female boomer children. According to the Bureau of Labor Statistics, the labor participation rate of women 55 years of age and older is expected to increase to nearly 40% by 2020, a rate higher than that of prior decades (Toossi, 2012). This is, of course, the prime age group for family caregiving (Redfoot et al., 2013). By 2030 even more will be faced with balancing caregiving and a full-time job.

Summary

There will be fewer family caregivers in 2030–2050 and most will be the adult children of boomers. The wealth of boomers has been overestimated, however, and many will fall short of having the resources to pay for daily care when they need it. Making matters worse is the likelihood that their children will also be faced with financial problems. They will not be able to afford reducing their work hours to care for their parents and other relatives. Many will still be paying off student loans, for themselves and their children.

Although the children of boomers expect to care for their parents and are willing, their ability to contribute is questionable at best. In addition, many boomers did not have children and some are living alone due to divorce and other family circumstances. Some boomer children will not live near their parents as the workforce has become more nationalized and globalized.

These are among the factors that can turn a "problem" into a "crisis."

Chapter Two

Boomers are not all that healthy: Prospects for caregiving need

The extent and depth of the 2030 crisis will be determined by the extent and depth of boomer caregiving need when they become the oldest old. Most analysts believe that boomers will be, on average, healthier than previous generations due largely to declines in cardiovascular disease, pulmonary disease, and other chronic illnesses. They attribute this to a decline in smoking, advances in medical technology and procedures, and increased control of hypertension and atherosclerosis through medication. This leads to some optimism about long-term boomer health according to two possible scenarios.

The first scenario anticipates a decline in disability along with a shortening of the period of disability as boomers become the oldest old. They see a problem, but no major crisis, pointing out that disability in the oldest old has declined over the last 30 years and that, overall, those 45 to 65 years of age in 2010 and now moving into retirement are healthier, wealthier, and better educated than those at a similar age in prior cohorts. Wealth and education have historically been associated with better health and reduced disability risk (Adler & Newman, 2002).

The second scenario is also optimistic about boomer health and disability but sees caregiving need as more of a problem due, ironically, to the very ability of medicine to extend the lives of older adults, thus potentially lengthening any period of disability. Both scenarios are still very much concerned with the overall social and economic costs of long-term care in 2030–50, including the burden on families. They recognize that the sheer number of aging boomers will assure that prevalence of disability will be high even if incidence (the number of new cases in a given year) is low (Knickman & Snell, 2002).

The problem becomes a crisis under a third scenario, however. Even if retiring boomers are somewhat healthier than previous generations, this is likely to change as they become the oldest old. Evidence suggests that those conditions that generate the greatest care burden at age 80 and beyond will be worse for boomers. Dementia, mobility disorders, and general frailty syndrome, are major conditions that require round-the-clock care. When combined with extended lifespans, an acceleration in the incidence of these conditions will change a 2030 problem into a full-blown national crisis. The burden of caregiving will grow substantially, in number of disabled, severity of disability, and length of time needing care. This chapter takes an in-depth look at this scenario.

Boomers and dementia

Rising dementia disability will contribute most to the 2030 caregiving crisis. The number of people with Alzheimer's disease, vascular dementia, and other dementias, will grow as the large boomer cohort enters old age.

In 2010, the number of individuals over age 65 suffering from Alzheimer's disease was 4.7 million. Based on current trends, the number in 2030 is expected to be 8.4 million rising to 13.8 million in 2050 (Figure 3; Hebert et al., 2013). With Alzheimer's disease currently representing only about two-thirds of all dementias (Plassman et al., 2002), however, total dementia numbers may reach more than 17 million by 2050.

Since the growth rate of the oldest old boomer population will accelerate in 2030–2050, a higher percentage of living boomers during that period will suffer from dementia. According to the Alzheimer's Association (2015), about half of those with dementia will be 85 years of age and older in 2050, at least seven million people. Yet, dementia projections for 2030–2050 may be understated if boomers, as some suspect, will be less healthy in retirement than is currently assumed.

Figure 3. Projected number of people age 65 and older (total and by age group) in the U.S. population with Alzheimer's disease, 2010 to 2050.

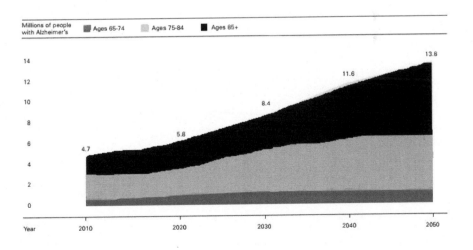

Source: Alzheimer's Association, *2015 Alzheimer's Disease Facts and Figures*, based on data from Hebert, L. et al, 2013. Reproduced with permission by the Alzheimer's Association.

Pre-boomer declines in dementia incidence

There have been a number of studies indicating that the incidence of dementia has been decreasing in pre-boomer cohorts. The studies show a decline in per capita diagnoses over the last few decades of the last century and the first decade of this century. The decline was between 30% and 50% depending on the time frame used and survey method (Larson & Langa, 2013). This has suggested that boomers may experience a similar decline or at least no increase in incidence.

The trend seems reasonably robust since it occurred even though lifespans grew during that time period and in spite of the fact that dementia has achieved a greater diagnostic profile over the last 30 years. Previously, dementia, or senility as it was called, was considered a normal part of advanced aging and typically not given much diagnostic consideration unless exhibited at a younger age. Any decline in new cases relative to population size is considered good news, even if the prevalence of the condition is still expected to rise as the huge boomer population enters old age (Hebert et al., 2013).

Although these studies were not designed to determine causes, researchers have pointed to two factors. One is that the studied cohorts have been, on average, better educated than prior cohorts. It is notable that those without a high school diploma in these studies did not show the incidence decline.

The second factor involves the known association of dementia with cardiovascular health, and with brain vascular health in particular, i.e., stroke risk. About 20% of all dementia cases are of the vascular type, and about 45% of Alzheimer's patients have "mixed dementia", that is, with vascular dementia as a co-morbidity (Nadeau, 2010). This means that more

than 50% of all dementia cases involve vascular factors. Vascular dementias are associated with stroke, from large-scale stroke to transient ischemic
events (mini-strokes) to so-called "silent strokes" involving micro-level
events in brain blood vessels. Hypertension and atherosclerosis are the
major direct risk factors for poor blood vessel health in the brain.

Since all forms of stroke have declined over recent decades (Koton
et al., 2014), it is reasonable to suppose that improved cardiovascular
health has contributed to the dementia decline. While it might be hoped
that exercise and better nutrition are behind these reduced cardiovascular disease impacts, the story appears to involve different factors: reduced
smoking and the use of medications to control blood pressure and atherosclerosis. Over the last 50 years, smoking has declined from 42.4% of high
school students and adults in 1965, to 19% in 2011 (Centers for Disease
Control and Prevention [CDC], 2013). A 50% reduction in stroke between
1987 and 2011, however, seems to be more closely associated with effective
treatment of high blood pressure and arterial plaque (Koton et al., 2014).

Retiring boomers may have an increased dementia risk

The decline in dementia incidence relates to pre-boomer cohorts.
Will this carry over to boomers? Many aspects of the boomer health profile at retirement point to a reversal of the decline including the following
worrisome trends in dementia risk factors:

Hypertension: According to the CDC, baby boomers 46 to 64 years
of age have higher rates of hypertension than did their parents' generation (Table 3). Although the percentage of boomers using medication
to control high blood pressure has increased, 35.4% compared to 23.2%

(King, Matheson, Chirina, Shanker, & Broman-Fulks, 2013), hypertension began at a much earlier age for boomers, due primarily to less exercise and higher levels of obesity at earlier ages (Leveille, Wee, & Iezzoni, 2005). The destructive effect of hypertension, including its impact on brain blood vessels, occurs across the lifespan (Allen et al., 2014; Iadecola & Davisson, R., 2008; Gorelick, P. et al., 2011). The sustained effects of hypertension on vascular health may have offset the effect of improved control of the condition through medication.

Hypercholesterolemia: The same CDC study reported that blood serum factors that promote arterial plaque are substantially higher in boomers than in previous generations (Table 3). Although the use of medications to control atherosclerosis risk factors has risen dramatically, from 1% to 25%, the risk factor still remains much higher for boomers (King, 2013). Like hypertension, this condition has its impact over a lifetime, quietly increasing plaque in blood vessels, including coronary arteries and brain blood vessels, potentially offsetting the impact of medication (Allen et al., 2014; Gorelick, P. et al., 2011). Again, less exercise and higher rates of obesity at earlier ages are implicated.

Diabetes and high blood sugar: Diabetes is a risk factor for dementia though the mechanism is not fully understood. Boomers at 45–64 years of age are more likely to have Type II diabetes than did those in the prior generation at the same age, 15.5% to 12.0% (King et al., 2013). The CDC (2010) expects the prevalence of diabetes to double or triple by 2050 depending on assumptions about incidence and mortality. Although more likely to have the condition under control, boomers appear to be pre-diabetic at a younger age, again due to obesity and lack of exercise. Recent studies have shown a connection between pre-diabetic high blood glucose levels and dementia, and even those higher on the normal blood sugar spectrum show a greater predisposition for dementia than those lower on the scale (Crane et al., 2013).

Table 3. Baby boomers compared to previous generation for hypertension and hypercholesterolemia.

	Hypertension (percent)		
	Previous generation 1988–94	Baby boomers 2009–2012	Percent increase
Males 45–64 years of age	34.2	42.2	23.4
Females 45–64 years of age	32.8	39.5	20.4
	Hypercholesterolemia* (percent)		
	Previous generation 1988–94	Baby boomers 2009–2012	Percent increase
Males 45–64 years of age	30.1	39.8	32.2
Females 45–64 years of age	36.4	42.4	16.4

Source: Based on data from the National Health and Nutrition Examination Survey (NHANES) of the CDC and available in their *Health, United States* 2012 and 2014 annual reports.

*Percent of population with hypercholesterolemia (serum total cholesterol greater than or equal to 240 mg/dl or taking cholesterol-lowering medications)

Boomers are more overweight and obese than previous generations (Table 4). Boomers have also exercised less than previous generations, and their lack of exercise has occurred over a much longer period of time. More than half of baby boomers 46 to 64 years of age reported no regular physical activity, compared to only 17% of the previous generation, and the percent of those who exercise at least 12 times per month was only 35% as compared to 50% for the previous generation (King et al., 2013). Thirty-eight percent are considered obese, based on the standard BMI index, compared to only 29.4% in the earlier cohort (King et al., 2013).

More importantly, boomers were sedentary and overweight at a much younger age. When members of the previous generation were 35 to 44 years of age, only 14–18% were considered obese. When boomers were between the ages of 35 and 44, the rate of obesity was 28–32%, almost double that of the previous generation (Leveille et al., 2005).

Mid-life obesity has been associated with increased dementia risk in several recent studies (Nepal, Brown, & Anstey, 2014). This lifelong life-style characteristic explains why dementia risk factors may have increased for boomers. While the use of medications may lower dementia risk, the silent damage to the brain vascular system over many decades may have already set the stage for an increased risk when they become the oldest old.

Table 4. Baby boomers compared to previous generation for obesity (BMI> 30)

	Obesity >30 BMI (percent)		
	Previous generation 1988–94	Baby boomers 2009–2012	Percent increase
Males 45–54 years of age	23.2	38.1	64.2
Females 45–54 years of age	32.4	38.3	18.2
Males 55–64 years of age	27.2	38.1	40.0
Females 55–64 years of age	33.7	42.9	27.3

Source: Based on data from the National Health and Nutrition Examination Survey (NHANES) of the CDC and available in their Health, United States 2012 and 2014 annual reports.

Other factors that point to a rising future incidence of dementia

Education level may not help: While higher education level has been associated with reduced dementia risk, it appears that the mechanism underlying the association may work against its importance. The prevailing theory as to why education has a protective effect suggests that education produces more neurons, more neuronal connections and synapses, and greater brain mass, a so-called cognitive reserve.

It appears, however, that this reserve does not combat brain processes that lead to dementia but rather delays the onset of dementia by providing alternative cognitive pathways to replace those that are damaged. Once dementia begins, however, it appears to accelerate faster in more educated individuals, canceling the benefit over the long run (Hall et al., 2007). In exchange for a later onset of dementia, therefore, the well-educated would expect to see their dementia become severe more quickly at the later age, in the middle of the 2030 crisis. While not necessarily adding to the overall burden, this suggests that higher education levels will lead to no significant relief, especially as life expectancy increases.

Chronic stress and depression: Recent studies have linked stress to dementia risk. While the mechanisms are not fully understood, cell and mouse studies have shown that sustained high cortisol levels generated by chronic stress increase the formation of amyloid-beta peptides, one of the primary ingredients in the sticky plaque that disrupts normal neuron function in Alzheimer's disease (Rosch, 2013).

Depression is also associated with an increased risk of dementia. People suffering from depression have more than double the risk for vascular dementia and a 65% higher risk for Alzheimer's disease (Wilson,

2014). Depression is related to chronic stress and those suffering from major depression or chronic depressive symptoms also show higher levels of cortisol which may be causing the increased risk. Some hypothesize that depression causes chronic inflammation and damage in brain blood vessels (Wilson et al., 2014).

Boomers experience more depression and chronic stress than previous generations (Kapes, 2013; McCarthy, 2015). The suicide rate of boomers between 1999 and 2010 was the highest of all the generational groups (Sullivan, Annest, Luo, Simon, & Dahlberg, 2013). There is good reason to think that damage has already been done to neuronal function and brain blood vessels in boomers, increasing the likelihood of dementia when they become the oldest old.

Reduced chronic disease mortality and increased years spent with dementia

Sixty-one percent of dementia patients develop three or more medical co-morbid chronic conditions that contribute to disability (Doraiswamy, Leon, Cummings, Marin, & Neumann, 2002). Many of these conditions can be life-threatening, including heart and vascular disease. Ninety percent develop psychiatric co-morbidities (Shub & Kunik, 2009). Improved treatment of co-morbidities has led to longer lifespans and will likely keep Alzheimer's patients alive longer in the future. Projections of future caregiving need must take this into consideration.

Those who argue for a likely compression of disability over coming decades point to recent successes in controlling chronic disease and the rising use of assistive technology. In the case of dementia, however, such success does not reduce caregiving need and, in fact, increases it. After 80 years of age, caregiving for a person with dementia goes well beyond the medical and becomes a matter of safety. Someone with moderate dementia at 80 years of age may be free of chronic disease and be able to walk without assistance, eat without assistance, and get in and out of bed without assistance. Though technically not disabled, they must still be watched closely.

Rising prevalence of dementia

"Incidence" refers to the number of new cases of a condition in a given period relative to a baseline population. "Prevalence" refers to the total number of cases of a condition at a given time in a given population. It is possible for prevalence to increase even while incidence decreases if the total number of new cases outstrips those cases that exit the system, in this case as a result of death. Thus even in the optimistic scenarios described above, dementia prevalence will grow through the 2030–2050. Those who do not foresee a crisis are arguing that it will grow at a slower rate (Knickman & Snell, 2002).

If incidence rates increase as a result of the risk factors described above, however, prevalence will grow more quickly than predicted. Underestimating the prevalence of dementia in 2030–2050 implies underestimating care need and caregiver burden. The Alzheimer's Association projects that there will be seven million boomer Alzheimer's disease patients 85 years of age and older by 2050. By adding in estimates for ages 80 to 84 (three million) and non-Alzheimer's dementia (another 3.3 million), a total 2050 dementia prevalence for those age 80 could reach 13.3 million. Even a small increase in incidence could bring this number closer to 14 million.

The overall prevalence of dementia is projected to triple by 2050. If we isolate the age 80+ population, however, the real growth may be closer to quadruple the prevalence. Nearly all of these cases will require round-the-clock care.

Dementia caregiving: The leading edge of the 2030 problem

As noted earlier, 14.9 million family and friends provided 17 billion hours of unpaid care to those with Alzheimer's and other dementias in 2013, averaging over 1,000 hours of care per caregiver per year. If dementia prevalence increases, all else being equal, even a conservative estimate of the increased caregiving need would put the number at over 50 billion hours of family care. With dementia care recognized as by far the most burdensome type of care for a family caregiver (Ory, Hoffman, Yee, Tennstedt, & Schulz, 1999), we see the true nature of the crisis we face and ask again: Who will provide this care?

Boomers and mobility disorders

The prevalence of dementia disability in old age will likely be amplified by the lifetime impact of chronic conditions like hypertension, diabetes, and stress overload. These conditions are due in large part to excess body weight associated with a modern lifestyle and workplace that are sedentary and conducive to increased consumption of high-calorie food. Excess body weight is also implicated in mobility disorders, another major source of disability and a likely second major driver of increased future caregiving need. In 2009, the Congressional Research Service expected 37.4% of those over 65 years of age to be obese in 2010. They projected that nearly 50% would be obese in 2030 (Sommers, 2009). This would make the boomers the heaviest generation of seniors in U.S. history, by far.

Mobility disorders are especially insidious since they tend to further reduce physical activity, which promotes even greater weight gain and musculoskeletal deterioration, a vicious cycle leading to the inability to perform important activities of daily living. With longer lifespans, the prospect of living for many years with a disabling mobility disorder could contribute significantly to the impending 2030 crisis.

Many boomers entering retirement overweight or obese have been overweight or obese from a younger age. This results in higher lifetime levels of mechanical stress placed on joints, tendons, and ligaments. While it remains to be seen to what extent this contributes to the overall level of disability when boomers become the oldest old, many predict a rising incidence and prevalence of key disabling mobility disorders including osteoarthritis, rheumatoid arthritis, and chronic back pain. We look at these disorders and other factors, and evaluate the potential of surgical procedures and assistive technology to ameliorate the problem.

Increasing osteoarthritis

Osteoarthritis (OA) is one of the most common causes of disability and care need. According to the CDC, 27 million adults had doctor-diagnosed OA in 2005 including 30.3% of those 45 to 64 years of age and 49.7% of those 65 years of age and older. Knee and hip OA, in particular, are major causes of disability and care need and the CDC reports that one in two develops knee OA by age 85 and one in four develops painful hip OA in their lifetime (CDC, 2014).

Obesity and lack of exercise can worsen the problem considerably. According to the CDC, two of three obese people will develop knee OA in their lifetime and 66% of adults with doctor-diagnosed OA are overweight or obese as compared to 53% of those without a diagnosis. Forty-four percent of adults with an arthritis diagnosis report no leisure physical activity compared to 36% of those without a diagnosis (CDC, 2014).

While doctor-diagnosed OA is not the same as OA that is clinically present with accompanying stiffness and pain, the general trend remains the same in the clinical case and the impact on active life expectancy, or life without disability, is expected to be significant. While years lived with disability increases with obesity or arthritis separately, according to a 2008 study, the combination of obesity and arthritis more than triples the number of years lived with disability requiring daily care. For men in this dual condition, 50% of the remaining years of life after 70 will be spent with disability, on average. For women, 60% of the remaining years of life after 70 will be spent with disability (Reynolds & McIlvane, 2008).

The CDC (2014) expects 67 million Americans over age 18 to have doctor-diagnosed OA by 2030. Given the large spike in prevalence that occurs after age 45, the obesity–OA connection serves to seriously challenge those who argue for a compression of disability as boomers become the oldest old.

Can osteoarthritis disability in boomers be controlled?

Osteoarthritis can be prevented or delayed with weight control and exercise. Those who already suffer from OA, however, have difficulty fighting disability. Studies have shown that weight loss alone, while helpful, does not reduce the pain of arthritis or increase functionality in a sustainable way due to continued inflammation. While exercise can help as well, studies have shown that a combination of weight loss and exercise can reduce inflammation as well as mechanical load and is much more effective than either weight loss or exercise alone (Messier et al., 2013). The difficulty in pursuing such a regimen outside a health facility, though, has forced many with knee and hip OA to consider joint replacement surgery instead.

The number of knee replacement surgeries tripled between 1993 and 2009 while the number of hip replacements doubled. According to a 2014 study, 95% of the growth in such surgeries can be attributed to the rise in the number of overweight and obese people (Derman, Fabricant, & David, 2014). This explains why the largest share of surgeries were for those under the age of 65, primarily middle-aged boomers seeking to maintain an active lifestyle (Derman et al., 2014).

There is no question that joint replacement surgery can mitigate the disability of boomers suffering from osteoarthritis and there will certainly be improvements in surgical technology over the next few decades. However, surgery does not erase all problems associated with OA. Many obese patients will not be candidates for such surgery for a variety of reasons and those who receive the surgery may find themselves with continuing pain, stiffness, and disability (Nicholson, 2013).

Fifty percent of knee replacement surgeries are for obese patients, but studies have shown that obesity is an independent risk factor for poor outcomes in knee replacement surgery (Nicholson, 2013). Post-operative pain is greater, recovery is slower, and such patients are at increased risk of complications. The likelihood of artificial joint degradation and early mechanical failure is also higher, with some needing more surgery in less than 10 years. Moreover, the surgery does not reduce the obesity that caused the initial joint pain, and without weight reduction and exercise, functional limitations may continue (Nicholson, 2013).

Clinicians are beginning to understand why outcomes are weaker for obese patients. In addition to the mechanical "wear and tear" aspect of OA, there appears to be a more significant cause of cartilage and connective tissue destruction. Adipose tissue, i.e., fat, is now recognized as an endocrine system of sorts, producing adipocytokines that can degrade joints and stimulate inflammation. Glucose and lipid metabolism play a role in this system. The propensity of the obese and overweight to have problems with glucose metabolism can lead to continuing post-operative inflammation (Sowers & Karvonen-Gutierrez, 2010). If an obese patient could not walk up a flight of stairs without pain and discomfort before surgery, the task can be nearly as difficult after surgery

OA does not affect only hips and knees. Hands, feet, other joints, and the spine are susceptible to OA and contribute to pain, discomfort, and disability. With inflammatory response of adipose tissue now seen as a major factor in all OA, boomers face an increase of OA in these areas as well.

Chronic back pain

Spinal osteoarthritis often leads to chronic back pain, another source of mobility disability and loss of capacity to carry out activities of daily life. Other conditions can also lead to chronic back pain in middle-aged and older adults, and complaints about such pain are already highly prevalent. By restricting activity and exercise, back pain can accelerate general musculoskeletal decline.

It is difficult to assess the prevalence of chronic back pain due to varying definitions of the condition and the involvement of many factors. Some researchers tend to emphasize occupational definitions and the loss of work time. Others see psychosocial factors contributing to the chronicity of pain. Since the pain is often intermittent, it is difficult to pin down exactly when back pain should be called chronic.

The general prevalence of chronic back pain among boomers, however defined, has already increased (Smith, Davis, Stano, & Whedon, 2013). There is also reason to suspect that boomers may see a rising incidence and prevalence of chronic back pain due to increases in several risk factors. The first is, again, obesity and the tendency of adipose tissue to promote musculoskeletal degeneration in osteoarthritis (Shiri, Karppinen, Leino-Arias, Solovieva, & Viikari-Juntura, 2010). The second relates to psychosocial factors, including anxiety, depression, and chronic stress. These are known risk factors for chronic back pain (Linton, 2000) and increasingly prevalent in boomers.

Increasing incidence of rheumatoid arthritis

Rheumatoid arthritis (RA) differs from OA in that it is an immune function disorder. The immune system attacks and degrades the body's joint cartilage with hands, wrists, elbows, feet, knees, and ankles most at risk. It affects women three times more than men and as many as 1.5 million people had RA in the United States in 2007 (CDC, 2014). More important, however, is a recent rise in incidence among women, following decades of decline. Preliminary studies suggest that obesity and metabolic disorders may be at work here as well. Adipocytokines are suspected of playing a role in either causing or enhancing the RA disorder (Crowson, Mattson, Davis, & Gabriel, 2013).

Given the large numbers of boomers and the large subset who are overweight or obese, even a modest impact on incidence can result in significantly increased prevalence of RA as boomers reach older ages. RA has no cure and its victims suffer extensive disability. Sixty percent of working age cases are unable to work after 10 years (Ruffing, & Bingham III, 2012).

Assistive technology and the risk of falling

We hear a great deal about technological solutions for the mobility impaired. Homes and apartments can be retrofitted with ramps, electric stair ascenders, handrails, shower seats, toilet seat risers and other devices. Walkers, wheelchairs, and scooters come in all shapes and sizes and can be of benefit to many. Some expect that technological development will significantly reduce the caregiving need of mobility-impaired older Americans.

It is unclear, however, if such technologies and their future versions will have much of an impact on the caregiving needs of the oldest old. The research is mixed, and many reviews of assistive technology show them as best for supplementing caregiving in the very old and severely disabled, not replacing it (Allen, Foster, & Berg, 2001; Anderson & Wiener, 2015). This is partly due to the common presence of those co-morbidities, such as dementia, congestive heart failure, poor vision, and frailty, which independently require caregiving. It is also due to safety considerations. An individual at high risk of falling, for example, may use a walker as an aid, but this can encourage the individual to maximize the benefit of the technology and potentially re-introduce the potential of falling.

To avoid a wheelchair, an older adult may underestimate her ability to move with an assistive device or handrail. Any rise in the number of people over 80 years of age living independently with assistive technology may leave many with an increased risk of falls.

Falls in the late stages of life are a major risk factor for profound morbidity or death. One-third of adults over 65 years of age fall each year and over 300,000 fracture a hip (CDC, 2015a). Between 25% and 75% of hip fracture patients are unable to function independently after one year (Magaziner et al., 2000). A hip fracture virtually guarantees placement in a nursing home for rehabilitation and may result in major orthopedic surgery or a significant increase in ongoing pain, stiffness, and incapacity. Hospitalization and rehabilitation stays due to falls are the largest single direct medical expense involving older adults, reaching $34 billion in 2013 (CDC, 2015b).

Safety is most important and cannot be sacrificed in an effort to incorporate assistive technology. Yet, those who would instead restrict activities or move very quickly to a wheelchair in the late stages of life would be no better off from the standpoint of care need. Unless provided with sustained physical therapy, a sedentary or wheelchair-bound older adult will quickly suffer muscle atrophy and further reductions in general functional ability, leading to an increase in the likelihood of institutionalization or the need for round-the-clock care at home. The imperative of preventing falls and their serious health consequences can therefore itself lead to further incapacity, greater caregiving need, and an increased likelihood of institutionalization (Tinetti, 2003).

Boomers and Frailty Syndrome

Many older adults with multiple chronic conditions are not frail and many frail elders do not have any chronic conditions. This has led investigators to consider frailty an independent medical condition leading to the emergence of a clinically-defined "frailty syndrome" over the last few decades.

Frailty is defined as a clinically recognizable state of increased vulnerability resulting from aging-related declines in reserve and function across multiple systems. Such decline affects the ability to cope with everyday stressors and acute illness. The ability of the body to produce energy, use energy, and repair itself is also compromised (Xue, 2011). After controlling for chronic conditions, it is estimated that 7–12% of older adults living in the community exhibit frailty syndrome including 25% of those over 80 years of age. Women over 80 years of age are 60% more susceptible than men (Xue, 2011). The percentage of nursing home residents exhibiting frailty is much higher.

The frailty vicious cycle

Clinicians diagnose frailty syndrome if three or more of the following are present (Fried et al., 2001):

- Muscle weakness
- Physical slowness
- Low physical activity
- Poor endurance and frequent exhaustion

- Unintended persistent weight loss

Most important, however, is the existence of a reasonably clear, self-re-inforcing cycle of decline with some hierarchical structure. The syndrome appears to start with muscle weakness and progresses through physical slowness and low physical activity (Xue, 2011). The combination of these factors then leads to a situation characterized by poor endurance and persistent weight loss. Research shows that the cycle holds independently of chronic conditions although they are usually present (Xue, 2011).

The vicious cycle appears to be bolstered by behavioral adaptions to declining reserves and capacity. As muscle weakness expresses itself, individuals react by reducing physical activity and confining themselves to an increasingly more limited "life space". They go out less frequently, avoid physical effort, and disengage socially. This, in turn, leads to further muscle atrophy, further reductions in activity, and a persistent sense of fatigue and exhaustion. Interest in food declines and weight loss can ensue (Xue, 2011).

Frailty in the community is not the same as disability and chronic illness, but it still leads to disability. When triggered by acute events such as falls, the condition can result in rapid deterioration and institutionalization. Frailty requires the investment of significant caregiving resources, potentially including round-the-clock hour care in the community.

Boomers, obesity, and frailty syndrome

Until recently, frailty syndrome was looked at in terms relating only to thin older adults and those exhibiting rapid weight loss. Over the last decade, however, the syndrome has been linked to obesity in older adults, especially women, and to physiological mechanisms triggered by excess weight. There are two main reasons for this inference. The first involves a mismatch between fat and muscle in overweight and obese people leading to decreased strength and increased mobility disability. This is called sarcopenic obesity and involves the replacement of muscle mass by fat (Blaum, Xue, Michelon, Semba, & Fried, 2005). The effect is greatest in obese older adults with excessive truncal fat, i.e., an extra-large waistline (Hubbard, Lang, Llewelyn, & Rockwood, 2010).

The second reason involves the presence of frailty inflammation biomarkers in obese older adults, along with low carotenoids. Inflammation and oxidative stress could explain the systemic deterioration in muscle function as well as the decline in other body systems in such "obese frailty" cases, though more research is needed to determine the precise physiological mechanisms (Blaum et al., 2005).

Mobility disorders will reinforce the vicious cycle of frailty. If excess weight and associated metabolic disorders are involved in the cycle, this would add to the future disability profile of the oldest boomers and put even further pressure on family caregivers.

Recent disability trends and unmet need

While it is still too early to speak definitively of a significant uptick in boomer disability as they reach the oldest old stage, it appears that further declines in disability are unlikely. To the contrary, disability prevalence may increase. A 2012 review of five national surveys made the following observations regarding trends during the first decade of the 21st century (Freedman et al., 2013). From 2000 to 2008, personal care need and activity limitations:

- continued to decline for those aged 85 years of age and older;
- remained flat for those between 65 and 84 years of age; and
- *increased* slightly for those 55 to 64 years of age.

The last group represents early boomers and the investigators noted the troubling possibility that the trend of steady decline may indeed be reversing with the boomer generation. While representing only a 1% increase over the same age group ten years earlier, this is significant for a middle-aged cohort (Freedman et al., 2013).

The review was unable to pinpoint any particular cause for this reversing trend over such a short period and investigators are taking a closer look. Earlier studies detecting a similar trend, however, linked it to obesity and to mobility disorders, diabetes, depression and other neurological conditions (Martin, Freedman, Schoeni, & Andreski, 2010; Seeman, Merkin, Crimmins, & Karlamanga, 2010). A 2012 French study of disability-free life expectancy supports this analysis. While the study did not see a negative trend in those already at age 65, it detected what they call "an unexpected expansion of disability" among adults 50 to 65 years of age, i.e., those of the boomer generation (Cambois, Blacier, & Robine, 2012).

A 2013 review of stroke incidence and mortality in Western Europe detected a similar trend. While stroke mortality rates declined continuously for adults 35 to 64 years of age between 1997 and 2005, stroke incidence did not decline at all and even rose slightly between 2002 and 2005 (Vaartjes, O'Flaherty, Capewell, Kapelle, & Bots (2013).

Unmet need

A further, often ignored, issue is unmet need. Because the U.S. does not have a long-term care system other than the Medicaid safety net, it is reasonable to expect that some care needs of the oldest old will go unmet. Researchers using the National Health and Aging Trends Study reported that 32% of adults over 65 years of age currently living in the community and needing help with ADLs, reported an adverse consequence due to unmet need over the course of one month (Freedman & Spillman, 2014). As many as 75% of those at the highest level of disability reported an adverse consequence and a surprising 60% of those receiving paid help in the community also report such effects. Minorities, low-income older adults, and those widowed or never married, had higher rates of adverse consequences (Freedman & Spillman, 2014).

The most common complaints were soiled clothing, having to stay in bed or inside, and medication errors, but the list of adverse effects included missed meals, inability to dress, lack of clean clothes, no hot meal, lack of personal or grocery necessities, and lack of showering or washing. The researchers also pointed out that these kinds of adverse effects were frequently implicated in falls, burns, hospitalizations, ER visits, nutritional deficiencies, and incontinence (Freedman & Spillman, 2014).

As the number of oldest old increases over the next decades and available informal caregiving declines, it is likely that, everything else being equal, the U.S. will see a rise in the prevalence of such adverse effects, both large and small.

Chapter Three

Emotional dimensions

ADLs include standard objective categories like dressing, bathing, self-feeding, functional mobility, personal hygiene/grooming, and toileting. For those living outside of a nursing home, there are additional so-called instrumental activities of daily living (IADLs), including shopping, money management, housekeeping, technology use, medication compliance, communication, and transportation. Sociologists and medical professionals use both categories to assess care needs and the extent to which they are met.

If objective ADL categories were the best way to evaluate care need for disabled older adults, then a nursing home would seem to be the ideal setting for caregiving. Traditional nursing homes are, after all, organized to meet these needs. Why, then, does no one want to put a disabled and/ or demented parent in a traditional nursing home until there is no other choice? Why would an adult child make such a huge personal sacrifice in order to avoid a nursing home for a parent?

Family caregivers know the answers to these questions. They recognize that strong psychological and emotional changes are occurring in their relative during the late stages of aging. Mild cognitive impairment progresses to full-fledged dementia. Walkers yield to wheelchairs. Congestive heart failure and muscle atrophy trigger the cycle of frailty. Minor urinary problems become incontinence. Falls trigger a host of physical and psychological effects. This descent into disability is accompanied by a loss of independence and control. It can lead to embarrassment and loss of dignity as others clean up after toileting accidents or hand feed those with weakness, arthritis, or tremors. Social interaction declines, reading and other intellectual activities are largely abandoned, and navigating the complexities of bureaucracy and money management becomes increasingly difficult. Such changes have powerful emotional consequences as new realities conflict with longstanding beliefs about personal identity and social role. It is understandable that physical deterioration is accompanied by a corresponding proliferation of mood and behavioral problems.

This reversal of roles and loss of self-identity adds an emotional dimension to the needs of older adults. This dimension is deep-seated and difficult to address in a traditional nursing home setting. Even those willing to enter a traditional home in order to avoid burdening their children, feel an immediate intensification of this loss upon entry. They look around and see the empty gazes of those who are older and more disengaged, and struggle to place themselves into this new reality. The sense of loss can be directly and indirectly communicated to close relations, often through erratic behavior accompanied by negative mood, delusion, anger, depression, and anxiety.

Nursing home staffs are too thin to address this dimension, already barely able to keep up with basic ADLs. Social workers and geriatric psychiatrists do not have the time to intervene in a sustained way. Family members wrestle with guilt and grief, often unfairly accusing the nursing home staff of neglect. Their own emotional burden often does not diminish after they are relieved of caregiving duties when a parent is institutionalized. To the contrary, the emotional burden on caregivers may even grow as they feel the need to show up daily at the nursing home, listen to angry complaints, advocate for the family member, and add a personal touch to an otherwise sterile environment.

This intuitive understanding of why a nursing home cannot meet the deeper emotional needs of a very old parent leads people to try hard to keep the parent in their own home or senior residence, or to move the parent in with them. What most disturbs a family caregiver and most contributes to a sense of burden is having to watch and deal with these emotional dimensions of aging. A full understanding of the 2030 crisis can only be had by appreciating what a family caregiver experiences when dealing with a declining family member on a daily basis.

Beyond ADLs: Negative mood and emotional distress in the oldest old

Family caregivers struggle to deal with their aging relative's mood disorders and emotional distress. Managing chronic illness, mobility problems, and especially dementia, would be more tolerable were it not for the affective dimension of care need (Table 5).

Table 5. Behavioral and psychological symptoms of dementia (BPSD)

- Agitation
  - Irritability
  - Aggression
  - Mood lability
  - Aberrant motor behavior
- Anxiety
- Apathy/Indifference
- Delusion
- Depressive symptoms/dysphoria
- Disinhibition
- Euphoria
- Hallucination
- Loss of Appetite
- Sleep disturbances
  - Insomnia
  - Sundowning
- Stereotyped behavior
  - Pacing
  - Wandering
  - Rummaging

Source: National Institute on Aging

Anxiety and worry in the very old

Older adults living in the community are generally satisfied with their lives. Surveys show that they are happier, on average, than younger cohorts (Yang, 2008), largely because they do not work, go to school, or have to deal with children. In addition, negative emotions are usually expressed passively and without the anger and distress found in younger adults. Such happiness actually increases with age, on average, and is not significantly affected by disability and chronic illness (Yang, 2008).

Yet passive acceptance of a life that requires little effort should not be confused with psychological well-being. Anxiety and worry are highly prevalent in older adults and can affect quality of life, especially for those already experiencing serious physical and mental decline. A 2011 study found that 37% of adults over 65 years of age worried at what the study called an "excessive" level, meaning excessive worrying for more days than not over six months (Golden et al., 2011). Twenty percent experienced excessive worry that was "uncontrolled", which is worry that returns repeatedly and cannot be stopped, and 6.3% had a clinical diagnosis of generalized anxiety disorder (GAD), a debilitating psychiatric condition. While these percentages drop by 25–30% by age 80, and even further by age 90, the numbers are high enough to be of concern when looking at the emotional life of older adults (Golden et al., 2011). All three severe worry/anxiety conditions are more prevalent in women.

These affective conditions are associated with decreased quality of life and increased co-morbid depression. Excessive worriers can suffer sleep disturbances, muscle tension, irritability, fatigue, and difficulty concentrating. Most of the worries, about health, family matters, personal finances, and crime, for instance, are of their own making, but are difficult to turn off (Golden et al., 2011).

High levels of worry and anxiety are also associated with cognitive decline, including mild cognitive impairment (MCI). While advanced Alzheimer's disease usually requires institutionalization, milder forms of memory loss and confusion are prevalent in community-dwelling older adults and prevalence increases with age. A 2004 study of patients with

MCI found that neuropsychiatric disturbances often accompany the impairment, including anxiety, which affected 25%, and irritability, which affected 29% (Hwang, Masterman, Ortiz, Fairbanks, & Cummings, 2004).

Diagnosing neuropsychiatric disorders in the very old is difficult given the natural cognitive decline in the aging process and the frequent presence of chronic medical conditions. Treating anxiety and excessive worrying at advanced ages is also problematic. Drug interactions and serious side effects, including further cognitive decline, limit the use of medicines that are used in younger populations (Cassidy & Rector, 2008). Psychotherapy is rarely prescribed though there are studies showing that cognitive behavioral therapy can address extreme anxiety in older adults (Cassidy & Rector, 2008).

Depression in the very old

Depression is also highly prevalent in older adults. Those experiencing serious physical and mental decline, or those who are alone for extended periods of time, are particularly susceptible. Depression can express itself as depressed mood, lack of interest or pleasure in activities, loss of concentration, lack of energy, guilt, feelings of worthlessness, difficulty making decisions, anorexia, weight loss, agitation or apathy, and suicidal ideation.

Although published rates vary, depending on definition, a 2003 review found that at least 13% of adults 85 years of age and older experienced clinically significant depressive symptoms (Blazer, 2003). Some have calculated rates that reach as high as 30% in long-term care facilities and as high as 40–60% for those with severe chronic illness (Birrer & Vermuri, 2004). These numbers get still higher if sub-clinical depression is also considered. Studies have shown that even such "subthreshold" depression can have negative behavioral impact and worsen functional limitations associated with chronic illness (Hybels, Pieper, & Blazer, 2009).

Clinical depression is generally underdiagnosed and often left untreated in older adults because many of the symptoms are also associated with chronic illness or the progression of dementia. Depression is also often co-morbid with anxiety disorders which share some common characteristics, including fatigue and poor sleep.

Agitation

Caregivers find agitation to be perhaps the most difficult of behavioral symptoms to address. Agitation refers to a range of behavioral disturbances including aggression, combativeness, shouting, hyperactivity, and disinhibition. Family caregivers can be especially burdened by verbal abuse and a lack of cooperation in the relative's own necessary care (Zal, 1999).

Agitation is typically a psychophysical expression of an underlying mood disorder, usually anxiety or depression. In the middle and advanced stages of dementia, however, agitation can be less self-conscious, more aggressive, and often fed by delusions. It is also more likely to be accompanied by odd behaviors including disrobing, walking into the street, throwing things, spitting, and attempting to phone the police or a dead parent. It can be caused or exacerbated by physical discomfort such as constipation, chronic pain, hunger, or extreme fatigue from sleeplessness. It can also be caused by certain drugs or drug-drug interactions.

Unfortunately, over 50% of dementia patients at the more advanced levels of disease exhibit some form of agitation (Zal, 1999). It is perhaps the most common cause of institutionalization and last-resort use of strong sedatives, anti-depressants, and anti-psychotics. These, in turn, can cause further mental and emotional deterioration even as they suppress the immediate troublesome behavior (Zal, 1999).

Boredom, sleeplessness, and chronic pain

The oldest old have diminished social networks. Friends and family members have died and illness and disability make social engagement difficult. They are often completely alone for long stretches, or for many days when living at home. Physical and mental decline tends to suppress the motivation needed to start new relationships, even in institutional settings, and television becomes the primary means by which the older adult engages with the world and accesses new experiences. Advanced dementia patients can become completely apathetic.

While television, meals, and family visits can occupy some of the time in the lives of the very old, in both the community and institutions, there are long stretches of time when little or no engagement occurs and functional limitations create a strait jacket of sorts. In addition to general loneliness, insomnia and other sleep disorders are common. Long hours may be spent trying to fall asleep or lying awake in the middle of the night. The increasing tendency to go to sleep early and wake early can create a tedious morning wait of many hours for those who need help getting out of bed, toileting, and preparing breakfast. The problem becomes critical in cases of sleep cycle reversal, or sundowning, where the older adult sleeps mostly during the day and is awake and restless most of the night (Fernandez, 2006).

A National Sleep Foundation poll in 1991 found that adults over 65 years of age had the highest rates of chronic insomnia of those polled (Ancoli-Israel & Roth, 1999). Insomnia and other sleep disorders can have a significant negative impact on health and well-being. Insomnia is a reason for falls. It is also reason for institutionalization as caregivers find themselves unable to cope with nightly sleep disruptions (McCall, 2004).

Several important mood problems can arise in such circumstances, going beyond the fatigue and loss of energy that accompanies poor sleep. The first is simply boredom. While not a clinical syndrome, boredom can have a significant impact on mood. Delusions and obsessions can proliferate and anxiety can be amplified. The mood-altering effects of chronic pain can also be amplified by insomnia. Older adults typically rate their chronic pain as mild or moderate when compared to the general population and are usually able to manage the pain through lifestyle and other adaptations. However, such pain can become a serious source of negative mood when it moves to center stage during periods of low or no social or other distracting activities, particularly at night.

Negative mood associated with boredom or chronic pain can lead to a worsening of chronic illness and accelerated mental decline. It can worsen day-to-day fatigue and weakness causing resistance to the kind of physical exercise and social engagement that can improve mood and slow physical and mental decline. It can also enhance agitation, anger, and disruptive behavior and the likelihood of developing major depression increases (McCall, 2004).

Unfortunately, pharmacological interventions for mild and moderate chronic pain (Molton & Terrill, 2014) and sleeplessness (McCall, 2004) are problematic at best in older patients. Drugs must be introduced with care and monitored for potential side effects, many of which can make a bad situation worse.

More years with emotional distress?

Family caregivers will delay institutionalization of a parent or other relative as long as possible. At the same time, medical advances are extending lives and reducing the effects of chronic physical disease. What is unclear, however, is the extent to which medical advances can delay or reduce emotional distress and mood disorders. The effects of long-term use of anti-depressants, anti-psychotics, and strong sedatives in older adults have been inadequately studied and preliminary indications are that such treatments have limited effectiveness beyond short-term use in extreme cases. They may even contribute to overall physical and mental decline (Zal, 1999).

Negative mood, behavioral disorders, and emotional distress will affect millions of the oldest old. Person-centered care in the community is best able to mitigate these psychological effects. However, if such care falls on the shoulders of family members, adult children in particular, there will be a price to pay in the form of caregiver burden and suffering.

Family caregiver burden

Older Americans and their families have been resisting nursing homes for years, but resistance is expected to be even greater for boomers. Gerontologists and advocates for the aging are demanding public policies that keep older adults in the community. Aging in place, preferably in the older adult's home, is dominating public policy discussions.

Unfortunately, the role of the family caregiver in this emerging environment is being taken for granted even as years spent with disability is projected to increase and the ratio of family members to aging boomers enters its projected precipitous decline. It is simply assumed that family caregivers, mostly adult children in 2030–2050, will take on the heavier burden. While advocates for caregivers seek support in the form of respite services, adult day care, counseling, and tax credits, they often do not fully appreciate the burden that comes with providing care for a disabled, aging family member experiencing chronic illness, dementia, mood disorders, and emotional distress.

Women in the workforce: The impact on caregiver stress

As noted in Chapter One, the financial standing of retiring boomers is likely to be weaker than expected and economic prospects for their children, GenXers and early Millennials, are not promising. These generations are marrying later and having children later, increasing the likelihood of having simultaneous responsibility for both parents and children, or "sandwiching". Given the widespread expectation that the social security system will face cutbacks over the next decades, including increases in retirement age, the combination of all these factors will force many boomer children to remain in the workforce longer than they had expected.

According to the Bureau of Labor Statistics (BLS), workers 55 years and older were only 12% of the workforce in 1999 but are projected to be 23.9% of the workforce, nearly one in four workers, by 2018. Significantly, women will be a major part of this trend. The Bureau projects that women 55 to 64 years of age will be an increasing segment of the workforce in 2020 even as numbers in other age groups decline (Toossi, 2012). They will be mostly the daughters of boomers.

Primary caregivers for older adults with daily care needs have historically been women: wives, sisters, daughters, and sometimes daughters-in-law. This has been a function of cultural norms and the more limited role played by women in the workforce in earlier times. According to a National Health and Aging Trends Study (NHATS), 62% of caregivers for older adults in 2011 were women. For the oldest old, the roles of wives and sisters diminish and the role of the daughter, when available, comes to the fore. Middle-aged women were the largest group of non-spouse caregivers in the study (Spillman et al., 2014).

The NHATS report also indicated that half of this large caregiver group of middle-aged women were working (Spillman et al., 2014). As women entered the workforce in large numbers over the last four decades, driven by personal interest or economic need, their role as caregivers began to change. They faced the challenge of simultaneously maintaining a professional career, or any full-time work, and caring for aging parents, uncles and aunts.

Women have not been entering the workforce gratuitously. The slowdown in the rate of productivity growth in the U.S. since 1970 and stagnating real wages since 1980 have made two-earner families the norm for maintaining a middle-class lifestyle, including putting children through college. This change in the employment of women has altered the caregiver role dramatically and has increased stress for women caregivers even as more men have become engaged in the caregiving process. The impact is being felt by male and female workers alike. According to an AARP report, 58% of all caregivers were in the workforce in 2012 (Williams, Devaux, Petrac, & Feinberg, 2012)

Family friction

Working women and men who assume major caregiving responsibility for a parent or other relative, find themselves assuming multiple roles. Tension can arise within a caregiver's family as less time is devoted to family matters, including leisure activities. The significant rise in the number of divorces, remarriages, and non-traditional families, among both boomers and their children, can add to the tension through complications arising from geographical dispersion and interfamilial relations.

Financial strain can also be a major source of friction as families face decisions involving financial support for an aging parent, the need for in-home resources, or transitioning to more advanced care in an institutional setting. In "sandwich" situations, there can be stressful debates concerning family priorities when college tuition for children, or the purchase of a first home or car, competes with financing long-term care. If a caregiver feels forced to leave the workforce, or switch from full-time to part-time work, family friction and caregiver stress can be further amplified as family finances decline. AARP reports that 10% of caregivers leave their jobs in order to care for an older relative, and those over 50 years of age lose about $300,000, on average, in lifetime earnings (Williams et al., 2012).

A 1999 survey of caregivers conducted for the MetLife Mature Market Institute revealed that 84% made formal changes to their working conditions in order to accommodate caregiving. Sixty-four percent took sick or personal days, 33% decreased their work hours, 22% used one or more leaves of absence, 20% changed from full to part-time status, and 13% retired early. 16% quit their jobs (National Alliance for Caregiving & National Center on Women and Aging at Brandeis University, 1999).

Workplace friction

Caregivers who cannot or will not leave the workforce, or reduce their work hours, face even more stress as they try to balance their care and work responsibilities. Caring for a parent is unlike caring for a child. Children are geographically close and their problems are generally predictable and manageable. Older adults are subject to erratic health and behavior patterns, sharp health changes and care transitions, and the unpredictability of acute care situations, including falls. Although some progressive companies provide an eldercare leave benefit, the United States overall provides perhaps the least private and public support for caregivers among the advanced nations (Arellano, 2015). Workers fend for themselves as they try to navigate the needs of their workplaces.

Employers may feel sympathy when the inevitable call comes from the ER after a fall, but sympathy can become frustration when the worker must help a parent move from ER to a hospital bed, then to the operating room, and finally the rehabilitation facility. Time spent comforting the parent and attending meetings with doctors and social workers can cause a significant loss of work time. When the parent finally is sent home, other problems may emerge if a home health or personal care aide is needed. Older adults frequently complain about aides and turnover is high. This all becomes even more problematic, of course, if the caregiver lives at some distance from the older adult.

It is common for caregivers to move into part-time work when such circumstances become the norm. Such a move, however, can have dire financial consequences. Part-time work is rarely compensated at anywhere near the level of a longstanding full-time position and comes with few benefits. There has also been a significant rise in the number of unmarried and divorced women who are sole earners and must stay in the workforce.

According to a recent survey, nearly 44% of women workers are the primary breadwinner in their family, including some in two-earner families (Prudential Life Insurance, 2014). Many are unmarried mothers or single. They typically have weaker support networks and face especially high levels of stress in caregiving circumstances.

Research has shown that employees with caregiving responsibility for a relative often face overt or subtle discrimination and harassment at work. AARP reports that lawsuits challenging employer actions against employees with family obligations are rising and that discrimination against women is often part of the problem (Williams et al., 2012). There are no federal or state laws that explicitly prohibit family responsibilities discrimination and caregivers who are treated unfairly must seek recourse through the ADA, or through age or gender discrimination laws, a difficult prospect (Williams et al., 2012).

These kinds of problems will most likely become worse over the next decades as the number of oldest old boomers grows, their degree of disability increases, and the number of available caregivers shrinks. Caregiver stress will deepen.

Caregiver depression

Becoming a caregiver for a disabled parent (or two) is a life-changing event and can cause significant emotional distress in the caregiver, expressed as anger, anxiety, and depression. The transition can cause or worsen two of the leading predictors of emotional distress in caregivers, *role captivity* and *role overload*, both of which can increase the prevalence of depression.

It is estimated that major depression runs more than twice as high among family caregivers as in the general population (Tennstedt, Cafferata, & Sullivan, 1992). Caregivers may also experience intermittent depressive symptomatology, which creates risk for further physical and mental health problems. Studies have reported general depressive symptoms in caregivers ranging from 20% to more than 50%, with caregivers of people with dementia at the higher end of the range (Tennstedt et al., 1992)

Caregiving is often characterized as a social "role". Pearlin and colleagues called it a "career" in a highly regarded series of studies in the 1980s and 90s of caregivers living with relatives who had dementia. In *Profiles in Caregiving: The Unexpected Career* (Anesbensel, Pearlin, Mullin. Zarit, & Whitlatch, 1995), they point out that the career begins at an unexpected time, involves tense interactions with family members, and develops a dynamic of its own, depending on factors rarely accounted for by the caregiver. The role emerges amid a swirl of emotions and life-changing decisions and must find its place in relation to other roles relating to family, community, and workplace, a process often fraught with tension and conflict, particularly when finances are an issue.

Powerful forces may lead to a feeling of role captivity, a sense of entrapment with no escape. To emphasize the potential for depressive effects, the Pearlin group asked dementia caregivers to respond to questions like "Do you wish you were free to lead a life of your own?" "Do you feel trapped by your (relative's) illness?" and "Do you wish you could just run away?" (Anesbensel, et al., 1995).

Role overload is an equally charged concept dominated by subjective descriptors like "overwhelmed" and "losing control", and psycho-physical effects including fatigue, poor sleep, and loss of appetite. The Pearlin survey asks caregivers to respond to statements like "You are exhausted when you go to sleep at night" "You have more things to do than you can handle" and "You don't have time just for yourself." (Anesbensel et al., 1995).

Role captivity and role overload can foster depressive symptoms and enhance the risk of major depression. They have the potential to overwhelm even caregivers with strong social support, high levels of education, ample financial resources, and a high degree of what the Pearlin group called "internal strength and mastery", the subjective sense of control in an important situation. For example, the Pearlin group found that caregivers with higher incomes and socioeconomic status experienced stronger feelings of role captivity, on average, than those with fewer resources (Anesbenel et al., 1995).

Impact of stress, anxiety, and depression on caregiver health and well-being

Much research has been done over the last few decades concerning the negative mental and physical health effects of family caregiving. Although more research is needed to establish strict cause and effect relationships, the initial findings of correlation are clear, as summarized in a 2008 review article (Schulz & Sherwood 2008). The article highlighted poor health behaviors and physical health effects:

Poor health behaviors: Caregivers are more likely to neglect their own health compared to non-caregivers, including poor eating habits, poor sleep, limited exercise, and failure to seek help with physical and psychological ailments. The neglect increases with the intensity and amount of caregiving, the level of disability, the extent of elder agitation and erratic behavior, and the extent to which the caregiver feels that the elder is suffering, physically or emotionally. It is highest in dementia cases that require constant vigilance. It is higher in caregivers with lower socio-economic status and fewer outside resources and support. It is higher in older caregivers who may ignore their own emerging chronic illnesses. It is higher when an older adult requiring intensive care resides with the care-giver, reducing respite opportunities.

Physical impact of emotional distress: Caregivers are often used as sub-jects in studies looking at the physical effects of chronic stress. Chronic stress elevates cortisol levels which can impact immune function and autonomic regulation. It can also lead to depression and anxiety disorders both of which can have impacts on physical health. The caregiving con-text can also add stressors from family tension and financial difficulties, as discussed above, further amplifying the level of stress involved. The lon-ger and more intense the caregiving experience, the greater the impact on caregiver health. Providing help that fails to improve the older adult's qual-ity of life further amplifies the effect.

Caregivers providing complex care

The desire to keep a disabled parent out of a nursing home can lead to a caregiver performing tasks that would normally be considered medical in nature and within the scope of professional nursing and home healthcare. This can add to caregiver stress and sense of burden.

An AARP/United Healthcare national survey found that 46% of fam-ily caregivers of older adults with multiple chronic conditions reported performing medical/nursing tasks. These tasks included: (1) manag-ing multiple medications, which could include intravenous fluids and injections (78%); (2) helping with mobility assistance devices (43%); (3)

preparing foods for special diets (41%); (4) providing wound care, including ostomy and changing post-surgical dressings (35%); and (5) operating specialized medical equipment, including ventilators and tube feeding systems (14%) (Reinhard, Levine, & Samis, 2012).

Operating medical equipment and providing wound care were considered the most challenging, yet fewer than 50% of those providing wound care, as an example, received training. Training was limited or non-existent for most of the other tasks as well. Caregivers felt they were faced with the fear of error and often struggled with lack of cooperation by the elder (Reinhard et al., 2012).

Fifty-seven percent of the surveyed caregivers felt pressured to take on these tasks and that they had no choice. Most felt they had a personal responsibility to take on these care activities because there was no one else to do it or because insurance did not cover it. Some felt pressure from the recipient or another family member (Reinhard et al., 2012).

Fifty-one percent of those surveyed felt their efforts were aimed at preventing nursing home placement and most were doing it despite the lack of home visits by a healthcare professional. There were no regular home visits in 69% of the cases. Fifty-three percent felt the need to become the primary coordinator of care and spent time talking to healthcare professionals and suppliers (Reinhard et al., 2012).

The surveyed caregivers reported feeling highly stressed. More than half reporting feeling "down", depressed, or hopeless within the prior two weeks. One third reported fair or poor health (Reinhard et al., 2012).

Summary

Chapter Two suggested that boomers will not see decreasing disability levels when they reach the oldest old stage and provided evidence suggesting that the incidence of disability may rise. The rise will be especially likely in the kinds of disability that create serious caregiving challenges, notably dementia, mobility impairment, frailty, diabetes, and neurological conditions including depression and anxiety.

This chapter suggests that these kinds of disabilities increase emotional distress in older adults and their sense of suffering. Emotional distress, in turn, advances functional disability in a vicious cycle. Longer life expectancies brought about by medical advances may have the unintended effect of extending the years in which the older adult is in distress.

Family caregivers struggle when watching a spouse or parent in distress or declining. This increases the physical burden on caregivers and deepens their subjective sense of burden. For adult children, getting heavily involved in care can mean a loss of income and increased family and workplace tension, further amplifying stress. Caregiver stress, in turn, can lead to poor health outcomes for the caregiver.

Increasing numbers of disabled boomers in 2030–2050, and decreasing availability of family caregivers, mostly adult children, portends a crisis. We need to seriously address ways to reform the U.S. long-term care system to ameliorate caregiver emotional burden. This will help not only caregivers and their families but will reduce the effect the crisis will have on the broader economy as fewer people will lose time at work or leave the workforce prematurely.

Chapter Four

Nursing homes

The Medicaid safety net serves as last resort support for indigent disabled older adults including those forced to spend down their savings to pay for extended long-term care. Beyond the safety net, and certain benefits available through the Veteran's Administration, there are only market-based, private-pay options and the informal care of family and friends.

The next four chapters describe the options for formal LTC in the U.S. and evaluate their current position and future trajectory in response to an aging society and the emerging caregiver crisis. They focus on the level of care that will be needed by the fast-growing population of oldest old boomers in 2030–2050. The next two chapters look at the current state and future potential of nursing homes, a sector that will necessarily play a major role. After that, community-based formal services are considered. Such services can be delivered in an assisted living facility or primary residence.

Overall, the current formal LTC framework will not provide much relief to family caregivers if extended to 2030 and beyond, and current projects and proposals aimed at improving the system are promising, but inadequate.

The state of U.S. nursing homes

After age 80, many older adults are faced with the prospect of entering a nursing home. Yet, nursing homes are anathema to boomers and their families. According to AARP, the age-adjusted rate of institutional use among older persons has already declined by 37% between 1984 and 2004, as previously noted, and the absolute number of older institutional residents has declined by nearly 600,000, or 29% from its highest level in 1989 (Redfoot & Houser, 2010). Only one sixth of the decline in institutional use can be attributed to declining disability rates; the rest reflects declining institutional use at every level of disability (Redfoot & Houser, 2010).

Correspondingly, older adults with disabilities are already increasingly living in the community, even at the highest levels of disability. According to the same report, the number of older adults needing assistance with two or more ADLs and living in the community increased by two thirds, nearly 1.2 million people, between 1984 and 2004 (Redfoot & Houser, 2010).

The resistance to placing older adults in nursing homes has worsened the quality of care in these facilities. State and federal budgeting for long-term care has begun tilting toward community-based care, leaving fewer government resources for improving nursing homes. There has been a "squeeze" on nursing homes as older, as previously discussed, as unsuitable facilities have been shuttered, private financing has dried up, Medicaid reimbursement levels have declined, and prospects for private payers have been impacted by the recession (Yoder, 2012).

Nursing homes hope to receive significant added funding for improvement in the face of a rapidly aging population. Yet, the politics of the situation makes this unlikely. Conservatives emphasize self-reliance and market solutions and want to curb social spending. Liberals are caught up in the community care and culture change movements and their promise of a more humane approach to caring for the oldest old.

While nursing homes receive diminished attention, the 2030 crisis will put millions of older adults without adequate financial resources or family caregiver options at their doorsteps. As discussed in Chapter Two, a large segment of those will suffer from dementia. This constitutes a major part of the challenge faced by the LTC system, and while dementia care will not be the only challenge, it is important to look closely at what dementia care requires. It is considered the most difficult and stressful of caregiving challenges (Ory et al., 1999) and a major reason for institutionalization.

Dementia care will drive an increase in demand for nursing home beds

According to the Alzheimer's Association, Alzheimer's disease (AD) patients will spend an average of 40% of their time with the condition in its most severe stage, a stage usually requiring institutionalization. Seventy-five percent of adults with AD are admitted to nursing homes by 80 years of age. Two thirds of AD patients die in nursing homes (Alzheimer's Association, 2015).

AD is by far the costliest of chronic conditions in the U.S., requiring an estimated $203 billion in care services in 2013, 70% of which was borne by Medicare and Medicaid. By 2050, the cost is expected to grow to at least $1.1 trillion (Alzheimer's Association, 2015).

Most moderate to advanced stage dementia patients are in nursing homes because family caregivers or senior residences, including assisted living facilities, are no longer able to provide the necessary level of care. This can be caused by the presence of co-morbidities requiring close medical attention. It is also due to safety concerns that can arise in the late stages of the disease and to the caregiver burnout that may result from dealing with AD behavioral problems:

Safety: Adults with moderate to severe AD are highly susceptible to accidents. Many can still walk and their memory loss, confusion, and delusions can lead to falls, fires, equipment malfunction, gas leaks and many other hazardous situations. The propensity to wander outside the house or climb over bed rails at night can create risky situations on the street and in the home. Toxic chemical ingestion and medication overdose are a further danger. Caregivers must be highly vigilant and patients must be constrained when warranted (Alzheimer's Association, 2014a).

Behavior: As discussed in Chapter Three, dementia patient behavior can be unpredictable and disruptive, even dangerous. Those with moderate to advanced disease may become bitterly angry, often for no reason, to the point of spitting, hitting, and throwing things, even when cared for by a loved one. They may make random telephone calls or walk off in an effort to visit a deceased parent. They may strip off clothing, curse, or exhibit other inappropriate behavior in social or public environments. They may repeat comments or questions for hours at a time. They can become morosely depressed or highly anxious for no apparent reason. They may categorically refuse food, medications, therapy, doctor visits, or toileting assistance (Llorente, 2013).

Such behavior is beyond what most assisted living facilities are licensed to handle. It is also beyond what a family caregiver can handle without putting personal physical and mental well-being at risk. If drugs are needed to control behavior problems, their use needs to be monitored closely by the skilled nursing personnel found in hospitals and nursing homes.

The surge in dementia prevalence will accelerate demand for nursing home beds over the next decades. Yet the strong movement toward community-based care and the weak current fiscal position of the federal and state agencies that support the nursing home sector raise serious questions about the ability of the nursing home industry to meet this demand.

Nursing home staff shortages, burnout, and turnover

It is difficult to measure or define nursing home quality. Most older adults do not want to be in a nursing home and feel a loss of dignity and independence upon entry. They start out, therefore, with a negative attitude. That attitude then rubs off on family members who wonder why their relative is complaining so much. Even after controlling for this problem, it is not uncommon to find two residents with opposite reactions to the same facility depending on the nature of their disabilities and their temperament, life experience, personal habits, and mental acuity (Vanderbilt Center for Quality Aging, 2013).

Staffing is one clear area of concern in the nursing home sector that transcends any particular facility and contributes most to negative perceptions and poor outcomes. LTC is first and foremost a human service, rendered by geriatric professionals but especially by direct care workers, mostly certified nurse aides (CNAs), who interact daily with the resident. Yet, inadequate levels of both professional staff and direct care staff are the rule in the industry. Burnout and turnover are endemic in the direct care workforce.

Direct care worker burnout and turnover

The regimented and sterile model of care that governs most nursing homes is driven by the staffing structure. Direct care staffing problems have to do with staffing numbers and ratios, but are primarily a function of low compensation, poor working conditions, and inadequate training, all of which contribute to burnout and high turnover, as follows:

Staffing ratios: There is no federal minimum direct care staff-to-resident ratio. The Nursing Home Reform Act of 1987 requires the presence of a nursing director with a Registered Nurse (RN) license for eight hours daily and RN or Licensed Practical Nurse (LPN) coverage for the remaining hours. Otherwise the Act states that the number of direct care workers must be "appropriate" for maintaining a high level of physical, mental, and psycho-social well-being of residents. Appropriateness is left to be measured indirectly, by monitoring for negative outcomes such as number of falls, prevalence of bed sores, resident complaints, unexplained deaths, use of anti-psychotic medications, and the like (Centers for Medicare and Medicaid Services, 2014).

When "appropriate" proved difficult to define, The Centers for Medicare and Medicaid Services (CMS) issued informal guidelines calling for a minimum of three hours of care per resident per day, roughly one hour by an RN and two hours by direct care workers. CMS also identified four hours per resident per day as optimal, with roughly three of those hours carried out by direct care workers (Harrington, 2002).

Most states have established minimum ratios but none that reach the four-hour recommendation for optimal care made by CMS.

When looked at from a caseload perspective, the same pattern holds. While a 5:1 ratio during the day for nurse aides is considered acceptable and caseloads exceeding seven may fail to meet need and prove distressing to the worker, a number of states have legislated minimum ratios of 8:1 with Texas requiring only 10:1 (Gregory, 2001). Some states have no minimum requirements. The national average CNA time per resident was about two hours per day in 1999 (Gregory, 2001), well below the CMS suggested optimum of three hours, and has grown only slightly since then.

Despite these poor staffing ratios, state interventions to assure appropriate staff levels typically occur only when poor outcomes are reported. While staffing levels must be reported to CMS as part of their nursing home rating system, a 2014 Center for Public Integrity study for the CMS showed widespread over-reporting of staffing levels, particularly in a number of southern states. Over 80% of nursing homes were over-reporting staffing levels (Lowenstein, 2014).

A particularly disturbing example of the impact of nursing home staffing shortages was revealed in a 2012 research project conducted by the Center for Aging at Vanderbilt University. The study observed the delivery of morning care over a four-hour period, once per week, for three months. The residents selected needed help with one or more of dressing, transfer out of bed, or incontinence care. High-rated and low-rated homes were chosen and staffing levels were at or above the national average (Simmons et al., 2012).

While aides generally responded to care requests, in 40% of the observations no care was requested and no care or communication occurred for the selected four morning hours each day despite the staff being aware that they were being observed. Those needing two workers for transfer were given the least attention. Some residents laid in bed with wet diapers. Others simply laid in bed while waiting to be directed by a staff member (Simmons et al., 2012). Leaving an incontinent resident unattended for more than two hours is considered clinically unacceptable and lengthy times in bed for any reason can cause or worsen depression, frailty, and other conditions, particularly bed sores (Getz, 2010).

Another study found that time in bed was directly related to staffing levels and that staff shortages could mean residents spending more than 18 hours in bed each day (Bates-Jensen, Schnelle, Alessi, Al-Samarrai, & Levy-Storms, 2004). In both studies, the passivity of residents played a role in the lack of care. Supervisors, however, were not enforcing required proactive protocols.

In 2015, CMS announced changes in its nursing home rating system requiring audited, payroll-based reporting of staff levels. Thirteen percent of nursing homes, about 2,000, will see their rating drop by 1–2 stars as a result of this change (Lowenstein, 2015).

While advocacy organizations are pushing nursing homes to achieve the 4-hour optimal level, there are deeper questions concerning the metric used to establish these levels. Such optimal level calculations address primarily safety and "objective" ADL needs of residents. The emotional needs of residents and family members are mentioned but given minimal consideration. Depression and anxiety, for example, are heavily treated with drugs. However, if non-drug therapy, including psychotherapy, exercise, and directed social activities, were used with or instead of drugs, as recommended by most geriatric psychiatrists, staff need would be correspondingly higher (Molinari et al., 2010). In addition, residents with dementia will typically need more than four hours of care per day.

Significant face-to-face attention is needed if a positive social-psychological environment is to be established, something critical to the emotional well-being of residents and to building a positive image for the facility. Staff shortfalls mean that the social-psychological dimension will tend to be ignored and psychoactive drugs will be more heavily relied upon as a method of dealing with psychological problems (Molinari et al., 2010). As emphasized in Chapter Three, however, meeting the emotional needs of the oldest old is an important and under-appreciated aspect of care. Failing to do so in an institutional setting will lead to continued resistance to institutionalization, and continued high levels of emotional burden for family members if they are forced to place a relative in a nursing home.

Nursing home owners and directors universally attribute shortfalls in staff-resident ratios and burdensome workloads for direct care workers to limited financial resources. They attribute financial problems mainly to cutbacks in Medicaid and Medicare reimbursements. The American Health Care Association reported that an 11% Medicaid cutback in 2011 cost the industry $6.3 billion, or $20 per Medicaid resident per day, the highest yearly loss to that point. In 2014, losses were $6.7 billion or $21.20 per resident per day, better than the 2013 shortfall but still problematic. The outlook for 2015 is somewhat improved due to an improving economy, but most expect growth in federal dollars for nursing homes to be modest, at best, and not enough to spur any sustained increase in nursing home budgets (Eljay LLC & Hansen Hunter & Co., 2015).

Financial excuses are greatest in the private sector where nursing homes focus on making a profit and higher executive compensation. Charging higher prices may limit competitiveness with assisted living and other community-based options (Yoder, 2012).

Burnout and turnover: Pay levels and working conditions for direct care workers are perhaps the most significant factors underlying quality issues affecting nursing homes. Poor pay and heavy workloads drive several vicious cycles. Burnout is common, leading to high turnover rates. Yet, turnover causes further workload increase as aides take on extra shifts while new aides, who do not start with heavy shifts, are hired and trained. In addition, high demand for direct care workers makes it easy for an unhappy worker to quit and move to another facility that may offer higher wages, better benefits, or commuting convenience. This can trigger a market-driven "revolving door" (Khatutsky et al., 2011).

Turnover also adds to budget concerns. It is estimated that it costs $3-4,000, on average, to replace a CNA (Castle, 2011). This is money that could have been used to improve the salaries and working conditions of existing workers.

High workloads and insufficient staff also add to on-the-job injuries, mostly associated with lifting and controlling residents. CNAs, the large majority of whom work in nursing homes, are age 39, on average, and should not be lifting residents alone (Khatutsky et al., 2011). Yet many have no choice. According to the CDC, one in five workers in the healthcare and social assistance industry reported non-fatal occupational injuries, the highest number reported for all private industries. CNAs and nurses had the highest rates among such workers, with nurse aide injuries running at double the rate of nurses (Gomaa et al., 2015).

According to a 2012 report, 60% of CNAs reported at least one non-minor workplace injury over the previous year, with 68% of those reporting more than one, for an average of 4.5 injuries per CNA. Eleven percent reported more than ten injuries. Nearly 50% of the injuries involved back injuries, other strained muscles, and bruises (Khatutsky, Wiener, Anderson, & Porell, 2012). Injuries contribute to absenteeism, burnout, and turnover and make it even more difficult to reduce the physical burden or increase pay (Table 6).

Table 6. Number and percentage of certified nursing assistants currently working in nursing homes who were injured at work in the past year, by type of injury received: United States, 2004–2005.

Work-related injuries	Nursing assistants working in nursing homes[1]	
	Number	Percent
Total[2]	680,800	100.0
Injured at work[3,4]	382,900	56.2
Type of injury		
Scratches, open wounds or cuts	302,200	44.4
Back injury	118,100	17.3
Black eyes or other bruising	109,600	16.1
Other strains or pulled muscles	106,400	15.6
Human bite	77,900	11.4
Other injury	48,700	7.2

Source: CDC 2004–05 National Nursing Assistant Survey (NNAS) prepared by the Division of Health Care Statistics, Long-Term Care Statistics Branch.

Notes: [1] Estimates exclude nursing assistants who terminated employment between the time of the 2004 National Nursing Home Survey and the 2004–2005 National Nursing Assistant Survey (NNAS). Estimates only those certified nursing assistants still employed by the same nursing home at the time of the 2004–2005 NNAS; [2] Includes unknowns; [3] Includes nursing assistants who were hurt or injured one or more times in the past year while at work. Injuries included reporting any of the following: back injuries, including pulled back muscles; other strains or pulled muscles; human bites; scratches, open wounds, or cuts; black eyes or other types of bruising; and other injuries from job; [4] If nursing assistant employed for less than 1 year, includes work-related injuries since nursing assistant began working at the facility.

According to the American Health Care Association, the median turnover rate (measured as the number of terminations over total staff) for CNAs in nursing homes was 51.5% in 2012, with rates much higher in some states (American Health Care Association, 2014). A 2012 report by the U.S. Department of Health and Human Services indicated that two thirds of CNAs who reported turnover in their facilities said that it interfered with their ability to do their jobs. Those who felt they did not have enough time to carry out their ADL responsibilities reported a higher likelihood that they would leave their job (Khatutsky et al., 2011)

Overall, one in four CNAs surveyed indicated that they were looking for another job. Between one third and one half said they were very or somewhat likely to leave their current job during the current year. Poor pay and finding a better job were the most common reasons for leaving and this despite the fact that CNAs reported relatively high overall satisfaction with their jobs (Khatutsky et al., 2011). The 2004–05 National Nursing Assistant Survey summarizes the various reasons for CNA turnover (Table 7).

These vicious cycles are continuing even as demand for direct care workers is rising at unprecedented rates and shortages are increasingly common. While this should lead to higher pay levels to attract new workers, there is little evidence to date that this is occurring. If it were to happen, however, the financial impact on companies would likely cause an even further increase in workload and further reductions in care services. It could also lead to the hiring of more workers with limited education, training, and experience, including immigrants whose communication skills are affected by English language deficiencies.

Direct care workers are extremely important in the nursing home environment. They are the primary interface between the institution and the resident and her family. Residents often become attached to an aide and agitated if aides frequently change. New aides must learn the resident's habits and preferences from scratch.

Table 7. Number and percentage of certified nursing assistants currently working in nursing homes who may leave facility in the next year, by major reasons given for leaving facility: U.S., 2004–2005

Major reasons for leaving facility	Nursing assistants who may leave facility[1,2]	
	Number	Percent
Total[3,4]	304,400	100
Poor pay..	113,100	37.2
Found a better or new job	87,200	28.6
Problem with facility policies or working conditions	47,600	15.6
Too many residents to care for	42,900	14.1
Poor benefits	33,500	11.0
Problem with supervisor	31,200	10.2
Moving out of area	23,900	7.8
Problem with coworkers	18,300	6.0
Other reason[5]	167,400	55.0

Source: CDC 2004–05 National Nursing Assistant Survey (NNAS) prepared by the Division of Health Care Statistics, Long-Term Care Statistics Branch.

Notes: [1] Estimates exclude nursing assistants who terminated employment between the time of the 2004 National Nursing Home Survey and the 2004–2005 National Nursing Assistant Survey (NNAS). Estimates only those certified nursing assistants still employed by the same nursing home at the time of the 2004–2005 NNAS. [2] Includes nursing assistants who responded "very likely" or "somewhat likely" to the following question, "How likely is it that you will leave your current job at [AGENCY] in the next year? Would you say very likely, somewhat likely, or not at all likely?" [3] Includes unknown reason. [4] Numbers will not add to total because a nursing assistant may be included in more than one category. [5] Includes all other reasons, including "problems with residents' families," "ill health," "child care issues," "care for elderly family member," and "problems with dying residents." None of these problems were reported frequently enough to meet standards for reliability and precision and thus are not reported individually.

Inadequate training: Only about 25% of nursing homes provide training programs for nurse aide certification. Most rely on training programs given at community centers, colleges, vocational schools, and hospitals. The Institute of Medicine, however, considers CNA training in geriatric care, and especially dementia care, to be inadequate and they recommend mandating additional curriculum components and expanding the minimum training hours to 120 (Wunderlich & Kohler, 2001). A review of outcomes for nine training programs that emphasized dementia care, found that eight of the programs led to improved patient outcomes and improved nurse aide job satisfaction (McCallion, Toseland, Lacey, & Banks, 1999).

AARP has strongly recommended that CNA training programs be updated to incorporate more units in the increasingly important areas of dementia, cognitive and behavioral disorders generally, catheter care, colostomy care, nutrition and feeding, hydration, and infusion therapy. They, too, recommend increasing the training minimum to 120 hours to include at least 50 hours in clinical practice (Hernández-Medina, Eaton, Hurd, & White, 2006). The federal government mandates a minimum of only 75 hours of study for certified nurse aides, 16 hours of which must be clinical training. Twenty-four states require only 75–85 hours of training and 17 states require only 16 hours of clinical training (Paraprofessional Healthcare Institute, 2014a). A report by the Institute for the Future of Aging Services points to a number of studies showing a positive relationship between the quality and quantity of training, and direct care worker turnover (Barbarotta, 2010).

Shortage of geriatric specialists

The United States is already experiencing a shortage of geriatric specialists and the problem will become more severe over the next few decades. This includes geriatricians, geriatric psychiatrists and psychologists, nurse practitioners with geriatrics training, and social workers with gerontology training. These shortages cut across all sectors of eldercare and are another source of dissatisfaction with institutional care, as follows:

Geriatric mental health services: Congress commissioned the Institute of Medicine (IoM) to study the healthcare needs of the older population as part of an effort to develop policy strategies. The first report in 2008 failed to deal with mental health issues, however, and the IoM was then asked to form a committee to look into that aspect of policy. In 2012, they published another report, dealing with mental health (Eden, Maslow, Le, & Blazer, Eds., 2012).

The report concluded that there was a serious and growing shortage of geriatrics-trained psychiatrists, psychologists, social workers, psychiatric nurses, mental health counselors, and substance abuse counselors. It also concluded that existing programs to increase the supply were inadequate and that regular physicians, nurses, and direct care workers were not receiving enough training in geriatrics and geriatric mental health to provide useful support (Eden et al., 2012).

Board certification in geriatric psychiatry has been available since 1991 and over 3,000 psychiatrists have received certification since then. According to the IoM report, however, the American Board of Psychiatry and Neurology indicated that only 1,382 certificates were still active as of 2010 (Eden et al., 2012). The report also stated that there was only one geriatric psychiatrist for every 23,000 adults 65 years of age and older, and suggested that ratio would become even less favorable as the population ages. With an estimated 14–20% of the population of older adults having at least one mental health or substance abuse problem, the potential scale of the future shortage is striking (Eden et al., 2012). Anxiety and depressive disorders are the most prevalent conditions driving the increase.

Interest in the subspecialty is in decline. According to the IoM, many of the 125–150 geriatric psychiatry fellowship slots go unfilled each year (Eden et al., 2012). Using data from the Accreditation Council for Graduate Medical Education and the Geriatrics Workforce Policy Studies Center, they report that fewer than half of fellowship slots were filled between 2006 and 2010. The 2011–12 fellowship number stood at only 58 (Eden et al., 2012). Having to undergo an additional year of residency at pay significantly lower than the pay of those who go on to regular medical practices has been part of the problem. In addition, limitations in Medicare and Medicaid reimbursement for geriatric mental health services has hit this area of medical practice especially hard (Eden et al., 2012).

Advanced practice nurses (APRNs) with specialties in gerontology and/or psychiatry are another important source of support for mental health services for older adults. The gerontology specialization curriculum includes core competencies in mental health management. However, only 2% of the quarter million APRNs in 2008 held this specialization and only one half of those worked full-time in this area of specialization. Only 4% of APRNs hold a psychiatric specialization (Eden et al., 2012).

The situation is similar for geropsychologists. This area of specialization was recognized by the American Psychological Association in 2010, having been only an "area of proficiency" up to that point. According to the IoM report, however, just 10-15% of graduate psychology programs offer a geropsychology track (Eden et al., 2012).

As of 2008, only 4.2% of practicing psychologists identified geropsychology as their primary focus of work and yet 39% of all psychologists report delivering services to adults over 65 years of age each week (Eden et al., 2012). This indicates a substantial and growing gap between specialty training and clinical practice in psychological services. In addition, as reported in the IoM study, the American Psychological Association indicated that only 16.3% of those identifying themselves as geropsychologists worked in nursing homes (Eden et al., 2012).

The John A. Hartford Foundation has conducted a number of reviews of research on the geriatric social work workforce. They report that in 2005, only 9% of social workers identified gerontology as their primary area of work and that 50% of master's degree-level social worker graduates said they had no interest in working with older adults. They also found that social workers who work with older adults were themselves typically older, with a median age of 50 at that time, including 10% who were ready to retire within two years (Council on Social Work Education, 2009). This will make it even more difficult to meet future demand. Using a 2004 Bureau of Labor Statistics projection, the Council on Social Work Education projects the number of social worker slots in long-term care settings to increase from 36,000 in 2002 to 55,000 in 2012 and to 109,000 by 2050 (Council on Social Work Education, 2009).

The shortage of gerontology-trained social workers is especially troubling because social workers for older adults engage in a good deal of care coordination including advance care planning, lifestyle transitions, and grief counseling. They can help navigate often complicated bureaucratic landscapes. They also interface with residents and family members and address emotional concerns.

The situation with licensed mental health counselors is even worse. Accreditation for gerontological counseling programs was dropped in 2009 and certification in gerontological counseling has been discontinued due to lack of interest (Bobby & Urofsky, 2008).

It is difficult to fully assess the shortage of professionals able to deal with geriatric mental health issues since many with knowledge and experience in this area do not necessarily possess certifications. Even when taking this into account, however, the IoM report firmly declares that "the rate of specialized providers entering the workforce is dwarfed by the pace at which the population is aging" (Eden et al., 2012, S-5).

Geriatrician shortage: The Affordable Care Act (ACA) promises to pay a 10% bonus in Medicare reimbursement for physicians who perform coordination of care services, something geriatricians are trained to do and expect to do. Certified geriatricians are also well-qualified to deal with the ongoing mental health issues of the older adults. The bonus is intended to attract more medical students into primary care and geriatric medicine by making up for the income shortfall experienced by such physicians. Although the program is still in its early stages, the results so far have been less than promising. Even fewer medical graduates elected to pursue a geriatric fellowship in 2011 (251) than in 2010 (279), despite the announcement of the ACA program (Langston, 2012). From 2000 to 2012, 25–46% of geriatric fellowship slots went unfilled (Eden et al., 2012).

As of 2012, the shortfall of geriatricians stood at about 10,000. The IoM and others project a shortfall of 26,000–30,000 geriatricians by 2030 (Eden et al., 2012). The size of the shortfall places it well beyond the number that might be coaxed into geriatrics by the ACA. The Hartford Foundation and several university consortia have begun providing geriatrics training to medical faculty in an effort to infuse the subject into the general curriculum (American Federation for Aging Research, no date). Since primary care physicians will be forced to take up the slack, this is sorely needed. However, medical schools are not currently set up to provide much in the way of clinical experiences in a long-term care setting (Buhr & Paniagua, 2011).

The impact of medical staff shortages in nursing homes

Most nursing homes cannot afford to have a physician, physician's assistant, or nurse practitioner on the premises as part of the permanent staff. This means that many residents are hospitalized when acute care situations arise. These situations include falls, pressure ulcers, dehydration, and so-called ambulatory care-sensitive diagnoses (ACSD) which can include flare-ups in conditions like asthma and diabetes. Hospitalizations are costly and most observers feel they occur far too often. The lack of available primary care providers, who might be able to diagnose and treat an urgent care situation, makes hospitalization more likely. Since Medicare picks up the cost of hospital stays and post-hospital rehabilitative services, there is little incentive for a nursing home to invest in on-site professional services.

A 2011 report by the National Consumer Voice for Quality Long-Term Care indicates that many acute care situations are preventable. They summarize research demonstrating that 10–25% of falls in long-term care facilities lead to fractures and lacerations. They also note that 20–30% of all falls in long-term care facilities are preventable without the use of restraints (Gallagher, 2011).

The same Consumer Voice report also cites research showing that pressure ulcers are endemic in some nursing homes, with prevalence reaching as high as 23.9%. Hospitalizations for pressure ulcers increased 27.2% between 1993 and 2006, a rate higher than the increase in all other hospitalizations (Gallagher, 2011). Yet pressure ulcer hospitalizations can also be prevented in the majority of cases through the use of preventative measures and effective treatment in the early stages. Such treatment, however, would require the availability of a physician or a wound-specialist nurse to carry out or supervise the process.

Nursing home residents are also frequently hospitalized for acute attacks associated with asthma, diabetes, congestive heart failure, and other ACSDs, reaching 45% of all hospitalizations in a Los Angeles study and as high as 67% in a study conducted in Georgia (Gallagher, 2011). Having a physician or other primary medical health provider consistently available has been shown to reduce the number of these hospitalizations (Gallagher, 2011).

Hospitalizations can also occur in cases of urinary incontinence, dehydration, and malnutrition. Many of these can also be prevented, but would require not only an available primary care provider but more direct care workers. Residents would need extra assistance with regular toileting or special attention paid to the feeding process and fluid intake. Current heavy direct care worker workloads make providing the extra assistance difficult.

Nursing home quality is evaluated mainly on the extent of poor outcomes. Hospitalizations due to falls, pressure ulcers, ACSDs, dehydration, malnutrition, and incontinence are a major consideration. While hospitalizations may be a valid indicator of quality, stepping up pressure for improved hospitalization outcomes without providing the physical and human resources to accomplish it can lead, perversely, to further overload and a worsening of nursing home staffing conditions. Numerous studies point to staffing as the central issue in trying to prevent hospitalizations as part of maintaining or increasing quality of care (Institute of Medicine, 2008).

Can nursing homes mitigate the family caregiver shortfall?

While characterizations of nursing home staff as uncaring are largely unfair, the objective circumstances in which they work may be responsible for this perception. Staff shortfalls, turnover, and poor working conditions have created the problem. A disabled older adult is going to react badly when asked to give up their comfortable and familiar home and community environment, regardless of the quality of the new environment. This negative attitude and current nursing home culture make for a toxic combination.

At the same time, the number of disabled older adults who cannot be cared for in the community will be growing rapidly and many of these will suffer from some form of dementia. The need for nursing homes will never be greater, but the industry, as currently constituted, will not be positioned to handle the need. Nursing homes are on the decline and there are shortages in many regions. Public funding has been stagnant at best and for-profit homes frequently compromise care through staff cuts in order to maintain business profitability as they compete with assisted living and residential care services.

Over the last few decades, reform efforts have arisen that hope to change the very nature of nursing homes. If older adults and their families can feel comfortable with the quality of nursing home care, this would help relieve the pressure on family caregivers, particularly those with the heaviest burden of care.

Chapter Five addresses the question: Can nursing homes be made more effective and hospitable?

Chapter Five

Prospects for nursing home reform

With long-term care moving inexorably toward community-based options, the future of nursing homes is very much in doubt as they compete for funding and public acceptance. Yet nursing homes will be the only option for many families as the caregiving crisis deepens and disabilities requiring intensive care become more prevalent. As family resources dwindle and private pay options in the community remain unaffordable, nursing home placement will be unavoidable for many. This chapter explores some innovations in the industry and assesses their ability to make nursing homes a source of mitigation for the 2030 crisis.

Dementia special care units

An increase in the prevalence of dementia in the oldest old will be a primary driver of renewed interest in nursing homes. According to the

Alzheimer's Association, over 60% of current nursing home residents have Alzheimer's disease or another dementia (Egge, 2013). The future of nursing homes is intimately connected to their ability to handle the rising number of dementia cases to the satisfaction of families.

Nursing home executives and dementia advocacy organizations anticipated this trend as early as the 1970s and 80s and experimented with special care units (SCUs) devoted to residents with moderate to advanced dementia. It has since caught on; of the 56% of nursing homes that provided dementia care in 2012, 55% used separate special units or wings, bringing the total portion of nursing homes with special dementia care units to 31%, nearly triple the portion reported in 1990 (MetLife Mature Market Institute, 2012; Holmes, 2015). These homes engage in heavy marketing to families, particularly those who can afford to pay privately, in an effort to gain an advantage in the otherwise declining competitive environment for nursing homes (Gruneir et al., 2007).

The recent growth of such units, and, in some cases, their higher price tag, has inevitably led to interest and concern by consumers and advocacy organizations. As a result, most states have introduced standards of care for such units and mechanisms for evaluation.

Standards for dementia SCUs

A 1992 report by the Technology Assessment Office of the U.S. Congress summarized the philosophy behind special dementia care units with six principles. According to a 2003 review article (Grande, 2003) they are:

- That something can be done for those with dementia.
- That the many factors leading to excess disability in dementia cases can be addressed.
- That those with dementia have residual strengths that can be encouraged.
- That behavioral issues in those with dementia are based on underlying real needs which can be addressed.
- That adjustments to the physical and social environment can positively affect an individual's functioning.
- That family involvement in care and care planning can positively affect both patient and family.

These philosophical principles have guided state efforts to establish standards of disclosure and regulation for SCUs. The Alzheimer's Association has since developed a similar set of principles. Regulations in Oregon closely reflect these principles and have served as a model for other states. A nursing home wishing to open an SCU, or what they refer to as a Memory Care Community, in Oregon must be endorsed by the state and provide written disclosure to prospective residents and their families of the standards the institution met to achieve the endorsement. These include the following elements (Oregon Department of Human Services, 2010):

Staffing: While the Oregon regulations do not specify a staffing ratio, SCUs are expected to meet the general licensing rules for nursing homes with staff "sufficient to meet the scheduled and unscheduled needs of residents." In addition, caregiving and non-caregiving staff must be trained "with a basic understanding and fundamental knowledge of the residents' emotional and unique healthcare needs," with the training conducted by individuals with experience and knowledge in caring for dementia residents. These pre-service and in-service training elements are listed in Table 8.

Assessment and care plan: Upon entry, the SCU must assess the resident and develop a detailed care plan that takes into account the interests of the resident, including customary routines, preferred activities, preferred meals, outdoor time, and other person-centered care aspects that encourage independence and preserve dignity. Table 9 provides an excerpt from the Oregon statute listing the key components of a comprehensive care plan.

Facility: Oregon has established a number of facility requirements that relate to the needs of dementia residents, including their emotional well-being. Table 10 provides a list of these requirements, as stated in the Oregon statute.

Table 8. Oregon memory care staff training requirements

	All Caregiving Staff	All Other Staff
Pre-Service Training Requirements	(1) The memory care community's philosophy that reflects a person directed approach that is related to the care of residents with dementia; (2) A description of the most common types of dementias and descriptions of disease process; (3) The need for careful diagnosis and available treatments; (4) The memory care community's policy and procedure on preventing elopement and procedures to follow in the event a resident elopes from the memory care community; (5) Environmental supports (e.g. staff interactions, lighting, room temperature, noise, etc.); and (6) Common behaviors and recommended interventions including: (a) Communication techniques that facilitate better resident-staff relations; (b) Approaches to implement with residents who have aggressive behavior, catastrophic reactions, and socially challenging behaviors; and (c) Providing personal care to an individual with dementia.	(1) The memory care community's philosophy that reflects a person directed approach that is related to the care of residents with dementia; (2) A description of the most common types of dementias and descriptions of disease process; (3) The need for careful diagnosis and available treatments; (4) The memory care community's policy and procedure on preventing elopement and procedures to follow in the event a resident elopes from the memory care community; (5) Environmental supports (e.g. staff interactions, lighting, room temperature, noise, etc.); and (6) Common behaviors and recommended interventions including: (a) Communication techniques that facilitate better resident-staff relations; and (b) Approaches to implement with residents who have aggressive behavior, catastrophic reactions, and socially challenging behaviors.

Required Training Within 30 Days of Hire	(1) Integrating leisure activities into the daily life of the resident; (2) How to evaluate behavior and what behaviors mean by observing, collecting information, and reporting behaviors that require on-going monitoring and possible assessment; (3) Family support and the role family may have in the care of the resident; and (4) Use of supportive devices with restraining qualities in memory care communities.	(1) Integrating leisure activities into the daily life of the resident; (2) How to evaluate behavior and what behaviors mean by observing, collecting information, and reporting behaviors that require on-going monitoring and possible assessment; and (3) Family support and the role family may have in the care of the resident.
In-Service Training	All caregiving staff must receive four hours of documented in-service training annually that pertains to the physical and emotional needs of residents with dementia. This is in addition to the licensing requirements for minimum in-service staffing. Training to address the behavioral or health care needs of specific residents that could be utilized with future residents may be counted.	

Source: *Chapter 411, Division 17, Oregon Administrative Rules,* Oregon Department of Human Services.

Table 9. Resident services in a memory care community: Care plan requirements

(1) Only individuals with a diagnosis of dementia who are in need of support for the progressive symptoms of dementia for physical safety, or physical or cognitive function may reside in a memory care community. Services must be delivered in a manner that promotes the autonomy and dignity of each resident, to maintain or enhance the resident's remaining abilities for self-care.

(2) At time of move-in, the community must make reasonable attempts to identify the customary routines of each resident and the resident's preferences in how services may be delivered. Minimum services … include:

(a) Assistance with activities of daily living that addresses the needs of each resident with dementia due to cognitive or physical limitations. These services must meet or be in addition to the requirements in the licensing rules for the facility. Services must be provided in a manner that promotes resident choice, dignity, and sustains the resident's abilities.

(b) Health care services provided in accordance with the licensing rules of the facility.

(c) A daily meal program for nutrition and hydration must be provided and available throughout each resident's awake hours. The individualized nutritional plan for each resident must be documented in the resident's service or care plan. In addition, the memory care community must:

(A) Provide visual contrast between plates, eating utensils, and the table to maximize the independence of each resident; and

(B) Provide adaptive eating utensils for those residents who have been evaluated as needing them to maintain their eating skills.

(d) Meaningful activities that promote or help sustain the physical and emotional well-being of residents. The activities must be person directed and available during residents' waking hours.

(A) Each resident must be evaluated for activities according to the licensing rules of the facility. In addition, the evaluation must address the following:

(i) Past and current interests;

(ii) Current abilities and skills;

(iii) Emotional and social needs and patterns;

(iv) Physical abilities and limitations;

(v) Adaptations necessary for the resident to participate; and (vi) Identification of activities for behavioral interventions.

(B) An individualized activity plan must be developed for each resident based on their activity evaluation. The plan must reflect the resident's activity preferences and needs.

(C) A selection of daily structured and non-structured activities must be provided and included on the resident's activity service or care plan as appropriate. Daily activity options based on resident evaluation may include but are not limited to:

(i) Occupation or chore-related tasks;

(ii) Scheduled and planned events (e.g. entertainment, outings);

(iii) Spontaneous activities for enjoyment or those that may help diffuse a behavior;

(iv) One to one activities that encourage positive relationships between residents and staff (e.g. life story, reminiscing, music);

(v) Spiritual, creative, and intellectual activities;

(vi) Sensory stimulation activities;

(vii) Physical activities that enhance or maintain a resident's ability to ambulate or move; and

(viii) Outdoor activities.

(e) Behavioral symptoms which negatively impact the resident and others in the community must be evaluated and included on the service or care plan. The memory care community must initiate and coordinate outside consultation or acute care when indicated.

(f) Support must be offered to family and other significant relationships on a regularly scheduled basis not less than quarterly. Examples in which support may be provided include support groups, community gatherings, social events, or meetings that address the needs of individual residents or their family or significant relationships.

(g) Access to secured outdoor space and walkways which allow residents to enter and return without staff assistance, except when indicated by OAR 411-057-0170(5)(e).

Source: Chapter 411, Division 17, Oregon Administrative Rules, Oregon Department of Human Services.

Table 10. Oregon memory care unit facility requirements: Physical design, environment, and safety

(1) It is the intent of these rules that the physical environment and design support the needs of individuals who are cognitively impaired. The physical environment should maximize functional abilities, accommodate behavior that is related to dementia, promote safety, enhance personal dignity, and encourage independence.

(2) BUILDING CODES. Each memory care community must meet the following building codes:

(a) Newly endorsed memory care communities must comply with the Oregon Structural Specialty Code (OSSC) SR-2 occupancy classification. If endorsed prior to the SR-2 requirement, the facility must comply with the building code in place at the time of original endorsement.

(b) Memory care communities must be located on the ground level of the building to ensure access to outdoor space and safe evacuation.

(3) LIGHTING.

(a) Research conducted in regards to lighting intensities has shown an impact on individuals with dementia. Lighting throughout the day or night may have an impact on an individual's functional abilities, as well as in mood and behavior. For communities that are in development or remodeling to new standards, the Division encourages facilities to review and implement the Recommended Practice for Lighting and Visual Environment for Senior Living as outlined in the ANSI/IESNA RP-28-07.

(b) The following lighting requirements must be met. These requirements apply to newly endorsed, constructed, or remodeled communities which have construction documents approved on or after November 1, 2010.

(A) Light fixtures must be designed to minimize direct glare (for example: indirect or diffused lighting). Bare light bulbs or tubes are not allowed;

(B) Lighting fixtures and circuitry must conform to lighting intensities shown in Table 2;

(C) Windows and skylights must be utilized to minimize the need for artificial light and to allow residents to experience the natural daylight cycle; and

(D) All windows must have coverings which diffuse daylight and minimize glare without blocking all light during the day. In addition, bedroom window coverings must provide privacy and block light from street lights or parking lot lights from entering the bedroom at night.

(4) SURFACE FINISHES. The following requirements for surface finishes must be met. These requirements apply to newly endorsed, constructed, or remodeled communities which have construction documents approved on or after November 1, 2010.

(a) Walls, floors, ceilings, and woodwork must be finished to minimize reflected glare and must have a low sheen or matte finish;

(b) There must be high visual surface contrasts to assist residents with limited visual acuity to distinguish between floor and wall, between wall and door, and between floor and other objects (e.g. toilet);

(c) Paint and other finishes used on the ceiling must have a light reflectance value of 80 percent or higher; and

(d) Paint and other finishes used on walls above 36 inches from the floor must have a light reflectance value of 60 percent or higher.

(5) SECURE OUTDOOR RECREATION AREA. The memory care community must comply with facility licensing requirements for outdoor recreation areas as well as the following standards. These requirements apply to newly endorsed, constructed, or remodeled communities which have construction documents approved on or after November 1, 2010 with the exception of subsections (d) and (e) of this section.

(a) The space must be a minimum of 600 square feet or 15 square feet per resident, whichever is greater and is exclusive of normal walkways and landscaping. The space must have a minimum dimension of 15 feet in any direction;

(b) Fences surrounding the perimeter of the outdoor recreation area must be no less than six feet in height, constructed to reduce the risk of resident elopement, and maintained in functional condition;

(c) Walkways must meet the accessibility requirements of the Oregon Structural Specialty Code. Walkway surfaces must be a medium to dark reflectance value to prevent glare from reflected sunlight;

(d) Outdoor furniture must be sufficient weight, stability, design, and be maintained to prevent resident injury or aid in elopement; and

(e) Doors to the outdoor recreation area may be locked during nighttime hours or during severe weather per facility policy.

(6) COMMON AREAS. Common areas must include the following requirements:

(a) Freedom of movement for the residents to common areas and to the residents' personal spaces;

(b) A multipurpose room for dining, group and individual activities, and family visits that complies with the facility licensing requirements for common space;

(c) Comfortable seating;

(d) Safe corridors and passageways through the common areas that are free of objects that may cause falls; and

(e) Windows or skylights that are at least as large as 12 percent of the square footage of the common area.

(7) A public address or intercom system is not required, however if one exists it must be used within the memory care community only for emergencies.

(8) RESIDENT ROOMS.

(a) Residents may not be locked out of or inside of their rooms at any time.

(b) Residents must be encouraged to decorate and furnish their rooms with personal items and furnishings based on the resident's needs, preferences, and appropriateness.

(c) The memory care community must individually identify residents' rooms to assist residents in recognizing their room.

(9) EXIT DOORS.

Locking devices used on exit doors, as approved by the Building Codes Agency and Fire Marshal having jurisdiction over the memory care community, must be electronic and release when the following occurs:

   (A) Upon activation of the fire alarm or sprinkler system;
   (B) Power failure to the facility; or (C) By activating a key button or key pad located at exits for routine use by staff for service.

(b) If the memory care community uses keypads to lock and unlock exits, then directions for the keypad code and their operation must be posted on the outside of the door to allow access to the unit. However, if all of the community is endorsed, then directions for the operation of the locks need not be posted on the outside of the door.

(c) Memory care communities may not have entrance and exit doors that are closed with non-electronic keyed locks. A door with a keyed lock may not be placed between a resident and the exit.

(d) If the memory care community does not post the code, the community must develop a policy or a system that allows for visitor entry.

Source: *Chapter 411, Division 17, Oregon Administrative Rules,* Oregon Department of Human Services.

Are dementia care units effective?

Most observers agree that the underlying philosophy and goals of SCUs are laudable. They also agree that positive outcomes are achievable when programs are implemented in accordance with the standards developed by the Alzheimer's Association and implemented by Oregon.

Early research on the effectiveness of the units has been mixed, however, and it has been difficult to point to any one factor that causes a unit to be effective or ineffective. It is also difficult to define the notion of a positive outcome for an SCU as a whole, since treatment resulting in a positive outcomes can vary from individual to individual. Use of anti-psychotic medication in an individual case may be necessary and can lead to a positive behavioral result, for example, while reduced use of such medications is otherwise viewed as a major positive outcome for the unit. Most dementia patients are placed in SCUs because they have the most intractable behavior problems, making it difficult to compare SCU and non-SCU treatment and outcomes.

There are additional factors that make evaluation difficult. The size of the unit and staff to resident ratios must be considered along with the overall quality of the nursing home. In addition, advanced dementia patients are often effectively in end-of-life care and some outcomes may be better evaluated using palliative care and hospice standards, including the use or non-use of feeding tubes, medications, and hospitalization (Cadigan, Grabowski, Givens, & Mitchell, 2012).

There are studies of SCUs that point to both positive and negative results with respect to some of the more objective evaluation criteria. A 2008 report indicated that residence in an SCU involved a reduced use of bed rails (Gruneir, Lapane, Miller, & Mor, 2008). While such rails are intended to prevent falls, in dementia cases they actually increase the risk of serious injury, including head trauma, as patients are more likely to attempt to climb over them. The study also found decreased use of feeding tubes and increased use of toileting plans that reduced the need for briefs or diapers, a quality-of-life indicator. However, the study also found that SCU residents were more likely to be on anti-psychotic drugs than dementia patients not in an SCU (Gruneir et al., 2008). The use of anti-psychotics has been particularly concerning to many because it is often associated with pacification and abandonment, though this association does not necessarily hold true on a case-by-case basis (Phillips, Sprye, Sloane, & Hawes, 2000).

Another study comparing SCU and non-SCU residents found that SCU residents were more likely to be treated for breathing difficulty, more likely to have an advance care directive, and less likely to be hospitalized; but also found that they were less likely to be treated for pain and more likely to develop pressure ulcers (Cadigan et al, 2012), although another study found that SCU residents developed fewer pressure ulcers (Luo, Fang, Liao, Elliot, & Zhang, 2010). Still another study showed higher quality of life ratings but lower mood scores, conflicting results even when controlling for depression (Abrahamson et al., 2012).

SCUs can improve resident, family, and staff emotional well-being

Caregivers do not experience much reduced emotional distress after placing a family member in a nursing home. This is caused by the perception that the relative is herself suffering in the institutional environment. There are reasons to believe, however, that well-designed SCUs can have a substantial positive effect on the emotional well-being of residents, staff, and family members.

The study that reported lower mood but higher quality of life provides an indication of how an SCU can address resident well-being. The study showed that reports of greater overall satisfaction were based on the residents having more meaningful activities, a better environment, and greater comfort and autonomy relative to dementia residents not in an SCU (Abrahamson et al., 2012). A follow-up study showed that the typically greater number of hours spent by SCU direct care workers with residents was also positively correlated with quality of life (Abrahamson et al., 2013).

Several studies looked at the relationship between staff and family members in SCUs. One surveyed the healthcare proxy, typically the family member most involved in care, and found greater satisfaction with the care being provided in SCUs when compared with the non-SCU nursing home environment (Cadigan et al., 2012). An earlier study found that family involvement in SCU care planning and in developing advance directives led to greater family satisfaction with both the dementia care process and end-of-life care (Engel, Kiely, & Mitchell, 2006).

SCUs are also more attentive to the physical environment of the care unit, as exemplified by the detailed facilities requirements of the Oregon regulations listed in Table 10. A 2014 study reported that dementia residents are sensitive to the physical environment and that home-like designs that reflect comfort and safety lead to wide range of better psycho-social outcomes (Marquardt, Bueter, & Motzek, 2014).

Perhaps the most important research results concern SCU staff satisfaction and turnover. While caring for dementia residents is highly stressful, studies show that staff satisfaction is higher, and the intention of quitting lower, in the SCU environment. One study attributes this to a better interpersonal environment, including more positive relationships with supervisors, co-workers, and especially families. Focused training in dementia care, including techniques for communicating with residents and families, appears to be a major reason for this positive result. It can also be attributed to greater consistency in the caring relationship between staff and resident (Robison & Pillemer, 2007).

The relative success of SCUs provides some optimism for the role of nursing homes in mitigating the caregiver crisis. Home care and assisted living are usually not suitable environments for most of those with moderate to advanced dementia, particularly those with severe behavioral issues. If SCUs can overcome some of the resistance to nursing home placement and address the emotional well-being of residents and families, policy initiatives and funding increases may follow.

As discussed in Chapter Four, however, Increasing staff numbers and ratios in SCUs would provide a further boost to outcomes, quality of care, and overall satisfaction. Increases would further reduce staff burnout and turnover, and provide even greater attention to residents and their families. Some facilities recognize that SCUs need a higher level of staffing but are concerned that the added financial stress would mean higher prices for these units or cutbacks in other areas. This, of course, would be counter-productive, particularly if staffing levels elsewhere in the institution came under even greater pressure.

State and federal regulation and control of nursing homes must be strengthened in order to fully realize the potential of SCUs. Studies show that opening a dementia care unit has a positive impact on private pay enrollments and overall occupancy levels (Castle, 2008). Facilities that use a dementia care SCU to attract new clients should therefore fully disclose their qualifications to manage an SCU as well as staffing levels and available services. They must then be held to the standards through frequent reviews and strict enforcement. The evaluation process must go beyond the standard objective ADL outcomes assessment and include on-site inspections and interviews with residents, staff, and families.

While nursing home troubles go beyond dementia care, failure to resolve dementia care issues will surely worsen the ability of this sector to play a role in addressing the 2030 family caregiver crisis. Dementia care involves some of the most critical determinant of care effectiveness, since dementia care must address the psycho-social needs of residents, their families, and direct care workers.

Can the culture change movement re-invent the nursing home?

The idea has been around for a long time, but there has been a sharp rise in interest over the last 20 years in "small home" approaches to skilled nursing care. The basic idea is to change the sterile, institutional culture of nursing facilities by making them more homelike and responsive to individual resident preferences and interests. The goals include a higher quality of life, improved medical outcomes, and greater satisfaction with care by residents and their families (Green House Project, 2015). A number of mostly non-profit organizations have been designing, building, and evaluating stand-alone small nursing home facilities since the late 1990s, with the Green House design, developed by geriatrician William Thomas and his Eden Alternative organization, among the most popular. Through 2015, 260 Green House homes have been built in 32 states with more being planned (Robert Wood Johnson Foundation, 2015a).

In addition, some existing nursing homes, also mostly non-profit, are planning to implement, or have implemented, culture change based on principles similar to the Green House model, such as those promoted by the Pioneer Network (2015a).

The Green House design

While there have been many designs used to develop small home facilities, the Green House has often served as a model. Green House homes typically have the following features (Nolan, 2012):

- A stand-alone facility, serving 10–12 residents, with the look and feel of a private home including a private bedroom and bathroom for each resident.

- A common space, or "hearth", connected directly to the private rooms, featuring a living room, open kitchen, and single large dining table that can accommodate residents and staff for meals, recreation, and meetings.

- Staffing by specially trained, cross-functional nurse aides reporting to the household instead of a department, and working in self-managed teams.

- Resident-directed scheduling and activities, based on personal desires and interests.

- A sense of community shaped by those who live there.

- A nearby support team consisting of a medical director, nursing director, nurses, therapists, social service providers, and dietary specialists working in partnership with the direct care staff.

Green House features may vary based on location, client characteristics, and state regulations and standards. Safety considerations may affect the type and use of kitchen facilities, for example, and urban settings may change the physical design and access to outdoor spaces. Staffing and resources can vary. The basic philosophy and structure, however, remains intact (Nolan, 2012).

Effectiveness of the Green House model

The culture change movement is quite new and most of the current stand-alone homes were built over the last 20 years. Consequently, not enough independent research has been done to draw firm conclusions about their effectiveness. Most research has been descriptive and conducted or sponsored by organizations that promote the new model, a source of bias. Research of this sort is also notoriously difficult since it relies heavily on subjective assessments and self-reporting from residents and family members, with limited research controls and minimal longitudinal data available to identify positive or negative trends. Comparative studies have difficulty controlling for differences in resident characteristics and available funding.

In addition, Green House residents are typically more affluent, with more private payers and fewer using Medicaid. Medicaid use in Green Houses and similar homes runs at about 40%, on average, while it reaches 60%, on average, in traditional homes (Zimmerman & Cohen, 2010). Many traditional nursing homes have over 80% Medicaid residents and advanced dementia is also far more prevalent in traditional nursing homes than in Green House homes (Kaiser Family Foundation, 2013; Zimmerman & Cohen, 2010).

Although there have been few outcomes studies that compare the Green House model with traditional settings, two studies reported better quality of life in 4 of 11 areas including privacy, dignity, autonomy, and food enjoyment. They also reported more nurse aide hours devoted to care, less decline in late life ADLs, and greater resident and family satisfaction. Health outcomes were inconsistent, but generally better (Zimmerman & Cohen, 2010).

While not an exactly comparable situation, a study comparing small group living facilities in Sweden (10 residents or fewer) with traditional nursing homes had similar results (Zimmerman & Cohen, 2010). They found that, over the course of a year, residents in the smaller settings had better preserved function, less aggressiveness, anxiety, and depression, and a lower use of neuroleptics, tranquilizers, and antibiotics. Staff were more in favor of independent activities for residents, were more satisfied, felt more strongly that they were providing quality care, and complained less often about a need to spend more time with residents (Zimmerman & Cohen, 2010). Another study showed that group living involved less family burden (Zimmerman & Cohen, 2010).

Overall, the outcomes trajectory for small nursing homes has been a good one and few would argue against the philosophy and values associated with the Green House model. There is some debate about the meaning of autonomy and individuality for the oldest old, especially for those suffering from dementia, and there is some concern for the safety of residents if a facility takes too strong a stand against restraints and medications or too lax a stand on resident use of kitchen facilities and other equipment (Nolan, 2012). These are matters that can be addressed, however, and do not reflect negatively on future potential.

In addition, the small home philosophy reflects the ethos of baby boomers and their children. Indeed, boomers have been directly and indirectly involved in the design, implementation, and advocacy for such homes through their influence on policy and their dominance in non-profit organizations and government agencies. This provides some optimism that LTC policy can change in this direction.

There are several ways that this movement can impact the caregiver crisis. The positive potential includes:

Reduced resident and family emotional distress: Families will accept institutionalization of a very old, disabled relative if they feel that the experience will be more than just waiting to die. By providing a home-like environment, paying close attention to resident needs, interests, and preferences, and by cultivating autonomy and community, this approach has the potential to reduce the negativity expressed by residents who need to be institutionalized and increase family satisfaction. It can allow a family caregiver to move toward institutionalization in a timely manner and with less emotional distress.

Reduced use of psychoactive medication and restraints: The small home environment allows for experimenting with a greater degree of freedom for residents. Assuming that safety issues can be minimized, the Green House hearth design allows for easy transition between private and social environments. It also allows residents who have problems relating to others to develop schedules that avoid potentially negative interactions. This in turn reduces the need for physical restraints and psychoactive medicines.

Fewer hospitalizations: CNAs are integrated into the small home environment and can easily interface with residents. They are aware of the health status of residents and can detect and address problems in a timely manner. This provides the potential for fewer hospitalizations, particularly for those conditions that are sometimes associated with intentional or unintentional neglect in traditional nursing home environments, such as falls, pressure ulcers, malnutrition, and dehydration.

Green House and similar facilities can therefore help the nursing home re-establish itself as a serious care option for oldest old boomers. However, small skilled nursing facilities currently serve only a very small number of residents. As of 2015, there was one Green House bed for every 1,000 beds in traditional homes (Semuels, 2015). In addition, the homes are virtually all non-profit, and, given market and financial constraints, can operate only within a relatively narrow window of viability. The cost per bed to construct a facility is roughly double that of a traditional nursing home (Semuels, 2015) and the first homes were able to be developed only because they were provided grants from private foundations. The Robert Wood Johnson Foundation was instrumental in building the first homes through a 5-year, $10 million grant in 2005 (Green House Project, 2015).

They are also typically located in higher-income communities and rely more on private-pay residents who are younger and healthier, on average (Grabowski, Elliot, Leitzell, Cohen, & Zimmerman, 2014a). Private payers are needed for small homes because the current and future outlook for Medicaid reimbursement is not good.

Even strong advocates for the small home model recognize that start-up costs and the need for a higher resident socio-economic mix make it unlikely that the stand-alone Green House model can do much to relieve the impending caregiver crisis. They instead point to the promise of implementing culture change within traditional nursing homes (Centers for Medicare and Medicaid Services, 2015).

Can culture change work in traditional nursing homes?

The Pioneer Network is a group of culture change visionaries that was formed in 1997 and is now involved in major collaborations with the U.S. Department of Health and Human Services and the Robert Wood Johnson Foundation. The group serves as culture change consultant to traditional nursing homes nationwide. They have organized coalitions of stakeholders in over 30 states and have lobbied extensively for including culture change principles in state regulations and standards. They have also dispatched consulting teams to willing nursing homes to explain culture change and help in its implementation (Pioneer Network, 2015b).

CMS has responded to this advocacy by including culture change principles in its guidelines for institutions and the Affordable Care Act of 2010 makes explicit reference to the need to implement person-centered care at all levels of medical and long-term care. A major reassessment of nursing homes by the federal government is currently underway with a goal of updating nursing home regulations. Preliminary drafts show that "person-centered care" will be a significant feature (Centers for Medicare and Medicaid Services, 2015).

The Pioneer Network has adapted the Green House philosophy for implementation in large existing institutions. Their core principles are "choice, dignity, respect, self-determination, and purposeful living". They believe that "all elders are entitled to self-determination wherever they live" and that "community is the antidote to institutionalization" (Pioneer Network, 2015a).

In practice, these principles aim to counter the regimented approach of traditional nursing homes by encouraging teamwork, continuity, empowerment, and community-building activities, along with flexibility in scheduling based upon resident preferences. They also encourage less restrictive practices including minimizing use of psychoactive drugs and physical restraints, and modifications of the physical environment to promote culture change values (Pioneer Network, 2015a).

To date only a small number of traditional facilities, perhaps 13%, have implemented at least some of the reforms that meet Pioneer Network standards. However, like their stand-alone, small home counterparts, they are typically non-profit and less dependent on Medicaid. They also house younger and less disabled older adults, are better-staffed, and have access to greater resources, including capital for changes to the physical plant (Grabowski et al., 2014a).

A special 2014 culture change supplement of *The Gerontologist* included a meta-analysis of studies that compared existing nursing homes that had implemented aspects of culture change with those that had not, looking at a number of subjective and objective outcomes. The analysis showed that it was too early to draw many specific conclusions about what works and does not work in the new model. However, negative outcomes were rare and there were promising signs for positive outcomes (Shier, Khodyakov, Cohen, Zimmerman, & Saliba, 2014). While not decisive, a longitudinal study found that the culture change institutions experienced a 14.6% decrease in deficiency citations relative to comparison homes (Grabowski et al., 2014b). However, other studies indicated that culture change institutions did not show statistically significant improvement in health outcomes, or resident and family satisfaction (Bishop & Stone, 2014).

These tentative results raise significant questions: Can large institutions serving low-income and highly disabled residents implement culture change without a massive infusion of resources? Can partial or incremental implementation of culture change overcome the inertia of the prevailing institutional culture?

Resource requirements: Barriers to culture change in traditional nursing homes

Without waiting for more decisive research, major healthcare advocacy organizations are aboard and many states are now using the culture change model as the basis for LTC planning (Stone, R., Bryant, N.,

& Barbarotta, L., 2009). Rhode Island will not issue a license for a new nursing home unless it embodies culture change philosophy and design (Grabowski et al., 2014a) and other states are moving in this direction. The barriers to change are high, however, and it may be difficult to reform the current system without a significant infusion of resources.

The Green House developers built their homes from scratch to meet their ideal hearth layout. They argue that the effectiveness of their homes is a function of the synergistic interaction of the various aspects. According to them, the homelike environment is paramount, for example, and they emphasize the central importance of the hearth, including a kitchen, and its relation to flexible scheduling and community building. The Green House model also emphasizes the use of private rooms and baths that adjoin the hearth, and easy access to safe outdoor space. Nursing stations are eliminated and direct care staff facilities are woven into the fabric of the home. These changes to the layout were made to combat the sterility of the traditional nursing home. Similar changes would be needed in traditional nursing homes.

Retrofitting an existing large nursing home with kitchens, living rooms, linked private rooms and access to outdoor green spaces would be a major capital undertaking, one that few facilities are positioned to undertake (Grant, 2008). Can culture change proceed even without the physical features?

The Pioneer Network has interacted with traditional nursing homes on the assumption that culture change could be implemented even without major renovations. They argue that culture change is a state of mind more than anything else and can occur if the leadership and staff of an institution treat residents with a greater emphasis on person-centered care. They advocate for a focus on the values of respect, dignity, autonomy, choice, and community. This would require a different, less-hierarchical form of staff organization and greater emphasis on consistency of staff-resident-family interaction. Leadership and staff training would have priority.

The cost of implementing culture change at this level would not be overly prohibitive. Indeed, one of the largest for-profit chains of nursing homes, Beverly Healthcare, conducted several pilot projects with the help of culture change facilitators, at modest cost, mostly for training and consultant fees. Although their goal was to use culture change to improve their market position, studies showed positive findings in quality indicators for resident choice, autonomy, and dignity relative to other institutions owned by Beverly. Staff satisfaction with their work environment was also higher (Grant, 2008)

The early results did not improve the market or financial position for the culture change institutions, however, and although there might be longer term potential, there were no indications that the chain was ready to make large-scale capital investments in the physical facility (Grant, 2008).

The Beverly Healthcare pilot program, like the Green House and similar small home studies, also involved nursing homes with higher levels of resources and a lower dependency on Medicaid than the average nursing home. A more telling study involved homes serving a largely poor, urban community with a heavy reliance on Medicaid, and with poor quality ratings. The Promote Understanding, Leadership, and Learning Program, or PULL, initiated in 2010, involved Medicaid-dependent nursing homes from the Baltimore area. It was financed by the state of Maryland and a charitable foundation. The goal of the program was to introduce culture change principles without any significant capital investment (Eliopoulos, 2013a).

The PULL program approached 33 nursing homes in the Baltimore metropolitan area that were considered both under-performing (three stars or less on the CMS scale) and under-resourced (majority Medicaid financed). They were offered free on-site education and consulting aimed at improved quality outcomes based on culture change. Only 12 of the homes agreed to even meet with the project director, with 10 of them agreeing to participate. Reasons given for declining participation included inability to allow for the training due to inadequate staffing; belief that their current educational programming was sufficient; and the determination that they could not add any new initiatives at that time. There was also skepticism about culture change, particularly given limited Medicaid resources. Some called it a fad (Eliopoulos, 2013a).

The project was scheduled to run for 24 months, but, according to project leaders, the strategy had to be modified almost immediately due to barriers, including: lack of adequate clinical and managerial knowledge of the nursing staff; staffing patterns that did not include time for train-ing; lack of leadership support for training activities; and lack of the com-puters, DVD players, LCD projectors, and internet access, needed for the educational programs. They needed to secure time to bring leadership up to par in understanding culture change and even basic principles of effec-tive management. They also had to reorganize staff schedules and provide extra pay to bring direct care workers into the training process (Eliopoulos, 2013a).

Eight institutions managed to complete the program and a review of pre-test and post-test training results showed a 25% increase in knowledge of culture change principles. Five of the facilities showed improvements in overall nursing home ratings, two stayed the same, and one declined. Six showed improvements in staff quality, one remained the same, and one declined. In looking at defined quality measures, four showed improve-ment, and four remained the same (Eliopoulos 2013b).

Despite results showing some modest progress, the project leader expressed serious concern about the ability of such homes to implement culture change. Those institutions that responded well and showed improvement already had stronger and more progressive leadership, and a commitment to the process. This significantly influenced the course of the project. The homes that had minimal or no improvement were less committed to the program. Their leadership felt that the culture change training sessions were less important than training in important healthcare skills (Eliopoulos, 2013a).

The PULL program shows that homes with limited financial resources will have significant problems implementing even the basics of staff training in culture change. They will also need a significant upgrade in leadership. Faced with financial deficits due largely to inadequate levels of Medicaid reimbursement, leaders in these homes are understandably skeptical about being able to effect significant change, even in those areas not requiring capital improvements. Even allowing for improvements in some quality indicators, there will be little likelihood that residents or their families will feel differently upon entering such facilities. The PULL study makes no mention of any increase in resident or family satisfaction levels and it did not address staff turnover.

Effecting culture change in traditional nursing homes is a worthwhile effort. Research results, however, have not shown the kind of significant qualitative improvement needed to bring the nursing home into effective competition with community-based alternatives without an accompanying massive infusion of resources. Studies finding a positive direction were mostly conducted in institutions with greater resources and less dependency on Medicaid. Where Medicaid dependency was high, positive results only occurred where leadership commitment was high and after outside consultants found ways to overcome burdensome staff workloads and shortfalls in technology and staff knowledge.

In sum, it is unrealistic to expect culture change programs to effect more than minimal quality improvements in the large majority of nursing homes without a major commitment of financial resources. For culture change to make nursing homes into a viable long-term care option during the 2030 crisis, there will need to be:

- An investment into upgrading the knowledge and managerial skills of nursing home clinical and administrative staff.

- An increase in direct care workforce pay, benefits, and training, and a reduction in workload.

- A major capital investment in physically transforming nursing homes into more homelike environments. Without a private room, for example, the entire concept of culture change is placed into question. Yet the cost of providing a private room would be well out of reach for most facilities that currently use double-occupancy.

Sixty percent of nursing homes are for-profit. The Boards of these institutions will need to believe that this kind of investment into culture change is compatible with expected levels of executive compensation and corporate profit. For this to happen, non-profit homes will need to show the way, but in an era characterized by budget constraints and short-term thinking.

Nursing homes in 2030

Nursing homes are faced with many challenges. They are an expensive private pay option and must compete for public funding with community-based options. They are burdened with a negative image and public attention and government resources are increasingly directed to community-based options.

Most homes are seriously under-resourced and suffer the consequences of staff shortages, heavy workloads, and burn-out. Direct care workers, mostly CNAs, are among the lowest paid of any workers in the U.S. and have one of the highest turnover rates. The professional nursing staff at nursing homes have lower levels of nursing education and certification, and there are significant shortages of physicians, psychiatrists, psychologists, and social workers with knowledge and experience with older adults, as discussed in Chapter Four.

Special Care Units for dementia patients and Green House and similar small-scale homes have the potential to re-vitalize the nursing home as an LTC option, but the SCUs need more direct care staff to make a real difference and small homes appear unlikely to become more than a minor player. Attempts at culture change in traditional nursing homes suffer from resource shortfalls, staffing issues, and declining rates of government reimbursement. This is especially the case for large, Medicaid-dependent for-profit homes serving poorer and more disabled residents.

Congress has mandated that a nursing home bed must be offered to anyone at a high level of disability but without financial or family resources. This last resort approach to nursing homes will not solve the resource problem or improve the image of such facilities. Resources will be needed to create more SCUs and make them attractive to those whose loved ones suffer from dementia. More public support is needed to help traditional nursing homes become more hospitable through person-centered care.

Otherwise, many disabled older adults without family caregiving resources, or whose family caregivers cannot cope, will likely sit alone in their homes to avoid nursing home placement, well beyond the point where safety and health are compromised. This bleak future for aging boomers does not befit a modern nation.

Chapter Six

Assisted living

Nursing homes, even small homes using culture change principles, serve primarily older adults who are significantly disabled and unable to care for themselves. Most residents need 24-hour active or standby care at some level. According to the Kaiser Family Foundation (2013), in 2011, 63% of nursing home financing was through Medicaid, supporting low-income residents or those who have spent down most of their assets. Only 22% was through private pay. The remainder was paid through Medicare support for short-stay post-acute rehabilitation.

The average age of nursing home residents has grown over the last few decades, reinforcing the medical and institutional characteristics of this sector. Forty-six percent of nursing home residents were 85 years of age or older in 1997 compared to 40% in 1985 (Sahyoun et al., 2001). By 2005, 51.5% were 85 or older (Day, 2010). The increase has been due, in part, to the desire to delay nursing home placement as long as possible, and to medical advances that have increased the lifespan of those with serious conditions (Sahyoun et al., 2001; Day, 2010).

Disability levels in nursing homes have risen correspondingly. In 1985, about 50% of nursing home residents needed help with 5-6 activities of daily life. By 2004, the percentage had grown to 65% (Alecxih, 2006).

Nursing home operators, particularly those run on a for-profit basis, would like to attract younger and more able residents. However, the atmosphere created by the universality of walkers and wheelchairs, and the severity of disability, including extreme frailty and advanced stage dementia, keeps younger, more able-bodied people away. Despite no decrease in the number of those eligible, the nursing home population has declined. 4.5% of the older population were in a nursing home in 2000 compared to 3.1% in 2010, a 45% decline (West, Cole, Goodkind, & He, 2014). Even the percentage of oldest old in nursing homes, 85 years of age and older, declined between 1984 and 2004 (Redfoot & Houser, 2010). Most analysts see the nursing home population rising only if no other alternatives are available.

The following chapters discuss the role that the formal long-term care system plays in providing care to disabled older adults outside of nursing homes. This chapter discusses assisted living, a new and expanding industry. Chapter Seven discusses aging in place in a private residence. The goal is to determine the extent to which these options will mitigate the emerging caregiver crisis.

Assisted living and the oldest old

At least some of the decline in nursing home residency has been caused by older adults opting for assisted living facilities (ALFs) and senior residences offering similar services. Assisted living in particular has grown significantly as more families seek safe environments that provide meals,

24-hour awake staff, housekeeping, transportation, and a congenial social situation for an older relative. Most ALFs also can also coordinate care through contracts with personal care and home health service agencies to allow for scheduled and unscheduled support services, usually for an additional fee. They are designed as attractive residences, with lounges and gardens. They also promote themselves as guided by a person-centered philosophy of care.

ALFs serve very old adults including those with daily care needs. They differ from nursing homes primarily in the lack of skilled nursing care, including 24-hour RN, LPN, and CNA staff. They do not have the medical technology of a nursing home, do not dispense or inject medications, and cannot treat most chronic conditions.

The assisted living industry is of relatively recent origin but has experienced striking growth over the last 25 years. Although the definition of assisted living varies from state to state and it is difficult to get an exact number of residents, there were at least 750,000 living in such facilities in 2010, according to AARP (Mollica, Houser, & Ujvari, 2012). Others put the number closer to one million (Ortiz, 2010). Revenues for the industry grew from $42 billion in 2006 to $56 billion in 2011 (Kolus, 2012). While the 2008 recession caused a slowdown in industry growth and forced some providers into bankruptcy, the overall health of the sector remains strong (Ortiz, 2010).

Most of this growth is attributable to rising incomes and assets, at least through 2008. Part of this growth, however, can be attributed to the fact that government has been providing increasing support for community-based long-term care. Medicaid spending for community-based services has risen steadily over the last few decades as states have developed programs, mostly with federal Medicaid waivers, to support older adults in their homes and group residences, including assisted living. According to the Congressional Budget Office (CBO), Medicaid spending for nursing home care grew by 1% per year between 2002 and 2012 while Medicaid spending for community-based care grew by 8% per year. The CBO projects a 5.5% annual growth rate through 2023 (Congressional Budget Office, 2013) and, in 2010, nearly 20% of ALF residents received some Medicaid help with personal care and home health aide services, allowing an increasing number of these residents to age in place (Caffrey et al., 2012).

Like nursing homes, assisted living facilities serve the oldest old. In 2010, 54% of residents were 85 years of age or older (National Center for Assisted Living, no date). Although ALFs do not have skilled nursing care, many residents need help with ADLs. Thirty-eight percent of residents receive assistance with three or more ADLs including 72% needing help with bathing and 52% with dressing (Figure 4). The typical ALF resident also has 2–3 of the top 10 chronic conditions: high blood pressure (57%), some dementia (42%), heart disease (34%), depression (28%), and arthritis (27%) (Caffrey et al., 2012).

ALFs are primarily private pay options, however, and are mostly marketed to asset-rich older adults and those with long-term care insurance (Figure 5). Although not as expensive as a full-service nursing home, their cost is out of reach for the majority of older adults and their families, limiting their role in providing long-term care services (Golant, 2008). Lack of licensing to provide medical or skilled nursing care in most states further limits their growth. Nonetheless, the decline in disability and increase in active lifespans over the last few decades, as described in Chapter Two, has spurred growth in this sector. In addition, many of those with extensive disabilities, but without ongoing medical needs, can be managed in ALFs through contracted personal care and home health services. Family members often provide additional support.

Figure 4: Residential care residents receiving assistance with activities of daily living: U.S., 2010

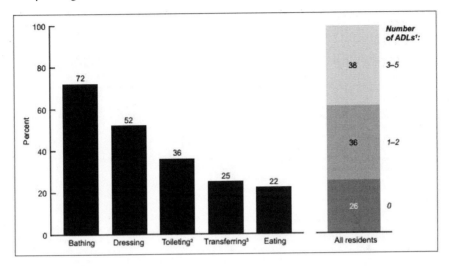

Source: CDC, National Center for Health Statistics, National Survey of Residential Care Facilities, Data Brief #91, 2012.

Notes: [1]Activities of daily living; [2]Includes 2% who receive assistance with a toileting device, such as ostomy, indwelling catheter, chairfast, or similar devices; [3]Comprises 12% confined to a bed or chair and 13% receiving assistance with transferring.

When it comes to the very disabled, Medicaid spending is still heavily weighted toward nursing homes. However, Medicaid policymakers understand that by funding personal care services that help with ADLs and provide some housekeeping, older adults can stay in an assisted living facility. Rising public support for providing long-term care services in community-based settings and the possibility that such services can reduce public spending on nursing homes has attracted the attention of owners of the ALFs, 82% of which are for-profit (Mollica, Houser, & Ujvari, 2012).

ALF owners are interested in growth and would like to serve a more diverse population. They are lobbying state governments to provide stronger financial support for residents with lower incomes and higher levels of disability. An industry increasingly dominated by large chains, ALF owners are developing business models that aim to produce positive outcomes at lower costs in an effort to attract the attention of state leaders (National Center for Assisted Living, 2015).

Figure 5. Estimated revenue sources for assisted living companies (2007)

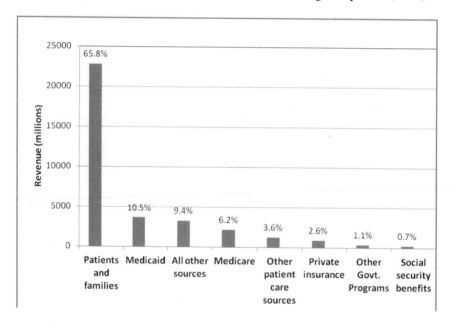

Source: 2007 estimated revenue sources for employer firms, U.S. Census.

They are also increasingly advertising the availability of environments designed to serve those with dementia, but without significant medical co-morbidities. A 2006 study reported that 48% of ALFs claimed to have some dementia-related care (MetLife Mature Market Institute, 2006). The CDC reports that, in 2010, 17% of residential care communities even had dementia special care units, accounting for 13% of all residential care beds. These facilities were more likely to be chain-affiliated, however, and less likely to be certified for Medicaid services eligibility (Park-Lee, Sengupta, & Harris-Kojetin, 2013).

These efforts have put the ALF industry in direct competition with the nursing home industry. As nursing homes provide more SCUs and seek culture change to attract clients who might otherwise opt for assisted living, assisted living facilities are looking for ways to recruit those who might otherwise enter a nursing home.

Factors that will affect the future of assisted living

Most analysts find it difficult to predict the future role that assisted living will play as the population ages (Golant, 2008). There are some factors, though, that are likely to determine the direction of the industry:

Affordability: ALFs are already outside the price range of most older adults especially given the impact of the recession (Ortiz, 2010). As current ALF residents reach ages where more ancillary services are needed to help with disabilities, the added cost of such services to the resident will force faster asset liquidation and more transfers to nursing homes.

Resident mix: The more disabled the community in an ALF, the less attractive they are to younger and less disabled potential residents, as mentioned above. This may neutralize the business model by attracting fewer new residents or by forcing institutions into a two-tiered structure. One well-publicized attempt to create such a structure led to a successful lawsuit by residents who fought the division of an ALF into two dining rooms, one for those with high levels of disability and a second for those more abled. The effect was to forcefully break up couples and friendships. The facility argued it was a safety issue. The judge saw it as a marketing ploy (Span, 2015).

Regulation and quality: ALFs are a relatively recent development and are lightly regulated. This is because they were originally designed with a relatively healthy client in mind. As more severely disabled clients are served, regulations are being sought to assure safety and quality outcomes (Newcomer, Flores, & Hernandez, 2008). Yet, outcomes-based regulation will tend to make ALFs more like nursing homes as they try to control falls, hospitalizations, and the like. There will need to be care plans upon admission and criteria set for discharge. Movement in this regulatory direction will become more likely as Medicaid funding is made available to the ALF industry, but this will further contribute to the development of a two-tiered environment.

The extent of regulation will also depend on public perception of the quality of assisted living facilities. As a profit-driven industry with light regulation, ALFs have generated a fair number of complaints and bad press. In a 2012 Public Broadcasting System (PBS) Frontline story on assisted living facilities (PBS Frontline, 2013, July 30a), an expert was asked to assess the quality of the industry given its recent rapid growth. She pointed to a lack of meaningful quality data for the industry and was concerned about its growth and mission expansion in the light of this deficit. She was particularly concerned about staffing shortfalls and turnover, staff training, and health outcomes, particularly if the facility was not operating with a Medicaid waiver. Most states do not have an ALF quality rating system that could guide consumers. She noted that developing such a system would be problematic since there is still no clear definition of assisted living within and among states (PBS Frontline, 2013, July 30b).

The documentary also described a number of worst-case incidents involving facilities of the largest for-profit U.S. assisted living chain, Emeritus, including several deaths that were attributed to taking in residents too sick to be cared for or to inadequate staff training (PBS Frontline, 2013, July 30a). Negative publicity will be an important factor in determining the future of assisted living. The families of those who can afford such facilities are interested in quality issues and more likely to be aware of any bad news circulating about their local long-term care residences.

There is now a broad consensus that assisted living needs to be more tightly regulated (Newcomer, Flores, & Hernandez, 2008). Further regulation, if based on the nursing home model, will impact the industry by forcing it into more of an institutional framework. It could hurt corporate bottom lines as regulations start to define staff levels, training, and facility requirements.

Can assisted living mitigate the caregiver crisis?

The affordability issue makes it unlikely that the assisted living industry will do much to mitigate the impending caregiver crisis. Those who do not need a nursing home and can afford assisted living can already afford to have equivalent in-home caregiving services. This creates a zero-sum game as older adults with financial resources choose between the two modes of community-based care. While many will opt for an ALF, most will choose in-home care, for financial and personal reasons.

The affordability issue becomes even more problematic as state governments suffer budget shortfalls. Bound by law to provide last resort support for low-income disabled older adults, spending cannot be much further reduced for nursing homes as the boomer population ages. This can force reductions or flat spending on community-based LTC services in future decades.

Some are proposing that governments facilitate public-private partnerships between ALFs and public medical, housing, and LTC facilities and services, in an effort to provide enough cost reduction to attract more middle and working class residents (Center for Excellence in Assisted Living, 2014). These are residents who are not poor enough to benefit from Medicaid but not rich enough to afford private pay options. They are typically the most dependent on family caregiving. Expanding the LTC financing pool by incorporating government dollars from housing, hospitals, and other sectors does have some promise, particularly if, by doing so, costs can be reduced in those sectors. A partnership between an assisted living facility and a hospital, for example, could potentially reduce hospitalizations and acute care expenses paid for by Medicare.

Even if partnerships were established with other healthcare facilities receiving government dollars, quality issues would still have to be addressed. It will be years before states have regulations and processes in place that can objectively evaluate the quality of ALFs. It will take even more years to carry out evaluations and establish a research base. Government and public support will be needed if ALFs are to take on an expanded caregiving role. This support will not be forthcoming easily without some hard evidence that ALFs are doing a satisfactory job.

While ALFs are obviously popular, it will take much more to get older adults to leave their private homes and enter such facilities. There will be always be resistance to leaving a private home and entering *any* facility, even those with mahogany furniture and velvet drapes. One analyst remarked that ALFs were becoming "nursing homes with chandeliers" and doing little to reduce the negativity and emotional distress suffered by most who must undergo this kind of transition (Willgang, 2008).

Chapter Seven

Formal home care

Family caregivers may visit disabled parents in their homes, move in with them, or bring them into their own homes. Adding paid, formal assistance to this effort is helpful, whether it replaces some family care or supplements it. Formal in-home care can also help those older adults without family caregivers avoid or delay nursing home placement at a cost below that of assisted living facilities. As such, formal in-home help will be part of any amelioration of the 2030 crisis.

The desire to age in place at home is consistent with American boomer culture. Boomers place a higher value on home ownership and the automobile than prior generations. (Figure 6). Eighty-three percent of boomers live in suburbs or small towns (McGuckin & Lynott, 2012) and over 75% own their homes or apartments (National Association of Realtors, 2006). Although a large number of boomers grew up in cities, their parents led the postwar migration to the suburbs and have largely remained in the suburbs leading to a huge spike in car travel in the second half of the 20th century. Many of those living in cities also became homeowners during the wave of conversions of rental apartments to co-operatives and condominiums in the 1970s and 80s.

Figure 6. Percent homeownership rate: U.S. (1900–2010)

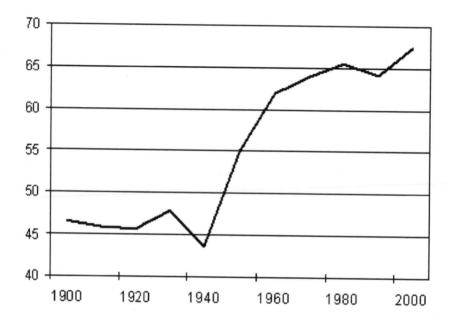

Source: U.S. Census

Boomers are particularly determined to drive and stay in their homes for as long as possible. Unlike many of their parents, they do not see institutionalization as inevitable. Since they also do not want to be a burden on their children, they will do whatever they can to stay independent and functional within their own homes and communities.

Boomers have not yet reached the oldest old stage but when they do, maintaining independence at that stage will be a serious challenge. Chapter One discussed the impending shortfall of family caregivers and the precarious social and economic conditions such caregivers, mainly adult children, will face. Chapter Two suggested that boomers may not be as healthy as hoped for due to obesity-related neurological and mobility impairments. Boomers will also be less financially secure than anticipated due to weaker than expected retirement finances and sustained economic stagnation in the U.S. and globally. The current economic environment has led to an almost universal obsession with cost-cutting and balanced budgets. It is unlikely that governments will promote expansive public spending on long-term care any time soon unless forced to do so by public political pressure.

Under these conditions, can the formal home care system provide the resources needed to care for the oldest old in their homes? What are the prospects for successful aging in place as we approach 2030?

Private pay options

Despite a weaker overall financial outlook, some boomers will have the resources to secure formal in-home services through private means, including long-term care insurance. These services can be used in conjunction with family caregivers or they can provide the bulk of care. As with assisted living and other residential communities that serve older adults, there is a wide spectrum of services that can be acquired depending on the nature and extent of disability. At the stage where assistance is needed with 2–3 ADLs, a medically-stable, non-demented older adult may need 8 hours or more of daily custodial care depending on the level of disability, degree of alertness, and availability of other help.

While custodial care workers can be hired directly, most beneficiaries contract with a home healthcare agency for a personal care assistant/aide

(PCA) on an hourly basis. Despite their uneven quality, agencies are a practical choice. They can offer replacements when there is a poor match and provide a substitute when an aide needs time off. They can also provide two aides if care is needed 7 days per week. Agencies also usually assume some supervision responsibilities and may provide training and other supports.

Although some agencies provide some training, there is generally no formal training requirement for PCAs and no licensing regulations. There are usually scope of care restrictions that prohibit agency PCAs from providing medical care. Many states designate home care workers who can provide basic medical care as home health aides (HHAs) and they usually must be trained and licensed. Definitions and training requirements vary from state to state.

Those with financial resources may hire PCAs or HHAs to care for a disabled older adult. Complementary resources that may also be available on a private pay basis including adult daycare, which provides social and cultural engagement for the older adult and relief for caregivers. A host of technologies can help elders in their daily activities including assistive devices for bathing, toileting, telephoning, moving around the home, transporting, cooking, and feeding. There are technologies that can help overcome hearing and vision loss, monitor vital signs, and alert emergency services. Homes can be reconstructed to include ramps, walk-in showers, bannisters, and other disability-friendly additions.

Being generally familiar with computers and the Internet, boomers with resources can also benefit from numerous online services including banking, bill-paying, shopping, investment management, and even medical vital sign monitoring. They will be able to access online communities, medical information, e-books, podcasts, and numerous sources of entertainment, news, and information, including hundreds of cable and satellite TV channels.

Older adults with sufficient personal or family financial resources may also elect to move to an aging-friendly residential community. Increasingly popular, these communities offer adapted homes or apartments equipped with assistive technologies. They usually have social activities, disability transport services, and a variety of community mutual help programs.

The cost of all this varies considerably. Having a PCA or HHA for 42–56 hours per week is equivalent to hiring a full-time employee. Adult daycare in more affluent communities can run as high as $150 per day, though the national average is closer to $70 per day (MetLife Mature Market Institute, 2012). Direct costs for formal home care will still be lower than assisted living in most cases.

The national average hourly rate for an agency PCA is $20, making the cost of eight hours of daily care about $58,000 annually. Rates can run as high as $40 per hour for agencies serving wealthier communities, however, bringing the cost to over $100,000 annually (MetLife Mature Market Institute, 2012). This is a considerable expense for even higher-income older adults and their families and shows just how difficult it will be for working and middle class families to afford such care.

Paying for complex care and round-the-clock care

The bigger problems for private pay care arise from the instability of late-stage aging. Falls are common even in the best of caregiving circumstances and often lead to surgery, rehabilitation therapy, and dramatic changes in health and disability status, including reduced mobility, increased frailty, and depression, as described in Chapter Three. In addition, chronic illnesses become increasingly worse over time, and episodes of acute illness are common, including urinary tract infections, dental infections, strokes, arrhythmias, and many others events that often require hospitalization. Sudden, destabilizing events can lead to a situation where older adults cannot return to their homes, at least not immediately, and a nursing home level of care becomes a necessity. Family members struggle to find alternatives under difficult circumstances.

In these cases, care gets increasingly medicalized and involves more frequent use of HHAs and regular visits by nurses, physical therapists, and occupational therapists. It also leads to more frequent visits to doctors and clinics for follow-up tests, monitoring, and medication adjustments.

For many aging adults, there will likely come a time when 8 hours of care is insufficient. Early morning care, including transfer out of bed, toileting, and feeding, becomes increasingly important for frail and disabled elders and is often needed as early as 5 or 6 AM. This could push care coverage into the 12–15 hour range daily if an aide is also needed to prepare the older adult for sleep. Costs for in-home care can become prohibitive, even for those with strong financial resources.

As discussed in Chapter Two, the expected substantial rise in dementia prevalence over the coming decades will further increase the scope and extent of caregiving need, with 24-hour care becoming a necessity in most cases. If accompanied by sleep and behavioral disorders or by medical co-morbidities, such care may even need to be fully alert and involve two shifts of awake caregivers. The cost factor then rises to even greater levels. The cost of live-in care can be as low as $150 per day. However, the average live-in daily rate for an agency personal care assistant carrying out intensive round-the-clock care is about $250, according to the 2012 MetLife Mature Market Survey. The cost gets higher for agencies serving wealthier communities. This can lead to an annual live-in direct cost of up to $150,000, not including meals and other services provided to the aide (MetLife Mature Market Institute, 2012). Such care may be needed for a long time should the effectiveness of medical treatment of chronic and acute disease continue to extend longevity.

The demise of the federal Community Living Assistance Services and Supports (CLASS) program

The vast majority of boomers will not be able to afford private pay LTC options for any meaningful length of time, especially when they became the oldest old and reach the highest levels of disability. They will then be faced with what many of their parents faced: forced impoverishment to achieve Medicaid eligibility.

During the lead-up to the passage of the Affordable Care Act, the case was made that, in addition to Medicaid, which targets the poor, the nation needed a universal long-term care insurance program that would cover the non-medical care needs of the disabled. This led to the passage of the Community Living Assistance Supports and Services Act (CLASS) as part of the ACA in 2010. The program would be available to all and paid for by participants through payroll deductions. Eligibility would be established after five years of payments and a cash benefit of up to $50 per day would be provided to an individual needing help with at least two ADLs. The benefit would have no lifetime limits and could be used for a nursing facility or in-home care (Colello & Mulvey, 2013).

CLASS was the culmination of a long history of attempts to get long-term care included in Medicare. There was, however, a major flaw in the program. Unlike the medical part of the ACA, participation in CLASS would be voluntary. This meant that adverse selection effects were inevitable. Those who were clearly going to need the program would enroll in large numbers, while healthier adults would opt out if they did not expect to need long-term care or did not see the $50 daily benefit as worth the investment, a problem that has dogged the private long-term care insurance market as well. Carriers would also be prohibited from rejecting applicants with a high risk of needing extensive care (Kapp, 2014).

CLASS was short-lived. By 2011, the Obama administration acknowledged that it had underestimated the extent of adverse selection. In 2013, the act was formally repealed by Congress. The more serious problem arose after repeal, however. Rather than redesign the program to make it mandatory, or expand federal financing of long-term care, Congress chose only to form a commission, to study the matter and make non-binding recommendations. As expected, the recommendations have been ignored by a fiscally timid Congress. Moreover, when addressing the funding issue, the majority of commission members preferred market-based solutions, with only limited public support, through tax credits, healthcare savings accounts, and other means. A call for expanded public financing for long-term care, by expanding Medicare or by other means, was supported by only a minority of Commission members. They argued that private approaches would not address the problem facing the millions who could not afford LTC and yet were not poor enough to access Medicaid (Long-Term Care Commission, 2013).

The failure of CLASS left only Medicaid, the program of last resort. Focus was shifted to efforts to include home and community-based services (HCBS) in Medicaid. A universal program that would include the middle classes was replaced by programs that would only kick in when an older adult became impoverished. Can Medicaid HCBS help mitigate the caregiver crisis?

HCBS services and disabled older adults

Medicaid was not originally intended to substitute for family care-giving in the community. It was created to provide a safety net for impoverished adults, at any age. It is a last resort for older adults lacking the financial and family resources needed to manage disabilities. Medicaid has a Congressional mandate to provide a nursing home bed for any impoverished adult needing one, including older adults.

As interest grew in home and community-based care, Medicaid began to offer options for HCBS. In 1999, the Supreme Court, in Olmstead v. L.C., ruled that forced institutionalization, at any age, was a form of discrimination under the Americans with Disabilities Act (ADA) and Medicaid was required to seek "least restrictive" alternatives to institutional care, if practical, and if the cost of such care was comparable.

The ruling provided a sharp boost to efforts to move away from nursing homes as the primary source of Medicaid long-term care. Initiatives commenced in a number of states driven by a desire to avoid ADA lawsuits but, more importantly, by increasing public interest and advocacy for HCBS services, for older adults and younger people with disabilities. There was also optimism that HCBS would prove to be less expensive than traditional nursing home care.

States developed a number of HCBS programs for older adults who would otherwise need a nursing home. Depending on the state, these included payments for basic housekeeping services, assistance with ADLs, assistive technology, care coordination, and simple medical tasks performed primarily by HHAs. Some states include funding that helped family caregivers directly through counseling, respite services, and even direct payment for providing ADL care. In addition, financial eligibility rules were relaxed in many states, allowing a higher income threshold for access to services and providing greater protection for assets in certain programs.

Between 1999 and 2008, Medicaid HCBS spending across the young and old disabled population grew by 153%, from $8.3 billion to $21 billion, a 96% increase. Over the same time period, Medicaid spending on nursing homes grew from a non-adjusted $39.4 billion to $49 billion, only 25%, and based almost entirely on increases in short-stay rehabilitation residents (Ng & Harrington, 2012).

There are three major types of HCBS programs in Medicaid:

- The Personal Care Services (PCS) program is largely used largely by older adults and provides mostly non-medical services including help with ADLs. Although only available in 32 states, it accounts for a large share of Medicaid HCBS expenditures for eldercare (Ng & Harrington, 2012). The use of this benefit has been uneven, however, with California and New York accounting for over half of PCS expenditures in 2008 (Engquist, Johnson, Lind, & Barnette, 2010). States are free to limit eligibility for this benefit and its scope (Ng & Harrington, 2012).

- The Medicaid Home Health program is an entitlement program that cannot be limited and must be offered to all eligible applicants. It keeps individuals out of nursing homes by providing home health aides, part-time nursing, and payment for medical supplies and equipment in cases where the provision of care in the home can be carried out in a safe manner. It is the smallest HCBS program usually serving as an add-on to Medicare- eligible services (Ng & Harrington, 2012).

- The HCBS waiver program under Section 1915(c) of the Social Security Act allows states to request a waiver of the nursing home-only requirement. Waivers must identify specific groups for eligibility, such as older adults or developmentally disabled younger adults, and participants must be functionally in need of nursing home care. Waivers are optional and states may restrict eligibility and the numbers served as they see fit. Services typically include case management, home modifications, and caregiver respite, although personal care services are included in some states. To qualify as a waiver, however, the program must be cost-neutral in terms of aggregate Medicaid spending. Over 70% of waivers target younger, mentally- and physically-disabled populations (Engquist et al., 2010).

Overall participation in HCBS programs grew from 1.6 million recipients in 1999 to 2.4 million in 2008 and 3.2 million in 2011. Expenditures for HCBS programs specifically targeting older adults grew by a remarkable 178% between 1999 and 2008 (Ng & Harrington, 2012).

The movement toward home and community-based care has been further bolstered by several provisions in the Affordable Care Act. Although participation is voluntary, they provide favorable reimbursement rates and other financial incentives for states that expand their HCBS offerings.

HCBS programs are now a permanent part of the Medicaid landscape and exist in one form or another in all 50 states. With their popularity and promise of cost savings, many feel they have the potential to play a major role in caring for boomers as they enter the late stages of life.

Constraints on Medicaid HCBS

Although the goals of Medicaid HCBS are widely endorsed, it is unclear if these programs can overcome the many barriers that constrain their ability to mitigate the caregiver crisis.

Funding constraints

Home-based care enjoys widespread bi-partisan support, but the collapse of the CLASS program points to the major obstacle for implementing any LTC program: funding. While it was expected that deficit hawks in Congress would find the program fiscally untenable, ACA proponents declined to press further for the financial resources needed to support a universal long-term care insurance program.

Federal funding is key, however, because states are required to balance their budgets and most states are in budgetary crisis. With powerful local political sentiment against raising taxes, most states have been averse to funding new initiatives and have instead been wrestling with how to cut public benefits and services, not expand them. Medicaid is only partially funded by the states, but states control the financial and management decision-making for HCBS programs.

States went into the HBCS process, however, amidst predictions that there would be significant cost savings, or at least cost-neutrality, as older adults chose the less expensive HCBS options that allowed them to live at home. The federal government was expecting the same. Unfortunately, overall cost savings have not occurred over the short run for most states and costs have even grown in many states. While there have been per capita savings relative to institutional care, it has been largely outpaced by growth in aggregate HCBS expenditures (Kaye, LaPlante, & Harrington, 2009). Although most analysts insist that there will be significant savings in the longer run, evidence for this has been mixed (Guo, 2014; Mollica, Kassner, Walker, & Houser, 2009).

While the Olmstead decision encouraged states to offer community options, it did not require anything specific and was written with the understanding that states would have wide latitude if they could not afford to expand offerings. The lack of short-term benefits has caused most states to implement fiscal controls on their HCBS programs. These have involved primarily (Ng, Harrington, Musuneci, & Reaves, 2014):

- *Increased financial eligibility standards*: Twenty-four percent of states reported using 1915(c) waiver criteria in 2013 that were more restrictive than those used for institutional care.

- *Increased functional eligibility criteria*: Ten states reported HCBS waivers that had stricter functional eligibility standards than those used by institutions.

- *Restrictions in personal care and home health services*: Twenty-one of the 32 states offering personal care services reported in 2013 that they had some form of cost control in place. Thirty of 50 states reported using cost controls in their state home health plan. The majority of controls involved reductions in allowable number of caregiving hours.

- *Reductions in provider reimbursement*: The same 2013 survey found that the hourly Medicaid reimbursement rate per visit declined for home health services and were flat for personal care services.

- *Use of managed care organizations (MCOs)*: MCOs can usually provide care at lower cost than standard Medicaid fee-for-service programs and some states are finding it more cost-effective to expand their state health plan home services programs even though they must accept all eligible applicants. Many are concerned, however, that MCOs achieve their lower cost by offering a lower level of care.

One effect of cost controls has been to limit participation in HCBS. This has led to the development of long and growing waiting lists for the programs. As of 2014, there were 536,000 on Medicaid HCBS program waiting lists with an average wait time of 29 months (Ng et al., 2014).

These cost-saving measures are not the full budget story. States are expected to carry out quality control monitoring and develop IT-based recordkeeping systems geared toward managing home-based care and providing agencies with meaningful data (Engquist et al., 2010). There is no central system, for example, to distinguish data relating to younger disabled adults from those relating to eldercare. Such efforts require significant investment, however, and have been neglected in most states (Office of the National Coordinator for Health Information Technology, 2013).

With respect to the PCS program there is the further problem of the number of allowable hours. Of the 32 states that have PCS programs, only about six allow more than 40 hours of care per week, an average of 6.7 hours per day on a 7-day basis. The rest offer hours that are so low that they will do little for those disabled boomers with few or no family caregiving resources (Kaiser Family Foundation, 2012).

Countervailing forces

The zero-sum logic of short-term budgetary thinking creates a number of unintended effects that will keep HCBS from meeting the expectations of its supporters. The main one has been dubbed the "woodwork effect" which suggests that as home-based services become available to disabled older adults, enrollments in these services will grow by attracting those who would not have otherwise entered a nursing home, creating a potential net increase in overall Medicaid costs. Since boomers will resist institutionalization at all costs, this effect may be quite large.

Fear of woodwork effects has spurred cost-containment measures in most states. Yet, to the extent that such measures restrict access to home care or reduce the amount offered, in the short run, the countervailing effect will be to drive even more aging adults into expensive institutional care. Cost-containment efforts may then, perversely, assure that potential long term cost savings will not materialize. For those remaining in the community, there will be even more pressure on beleaguered family caregivers.

There are other countervailing forces. Nursing homes have already begun protecting their own standing by lobbying for increased reimbursement rates and additional funds for culture change, special care units, and other services that will help them improve quality ratings and bring in more residents. They would also like to see financial eligibility criteria relaxed and made comparable to those used by HCBS waiver programs (McKnight's Long-Term Care News, 2012, September 11). This will counter the movement towards community-based care.

There is also a question of accountability for HCBS services, given a lack of formal standards of care. While nursing homes are audited and rated, home health agencies are only lightly regulated at both the state and federal levels (Graham, 2013). Assisted living facilities are facing greater scrutiny and there is every reason to expect that home care agencies will face the same, causing a slowdown in the rate of expansion of HCBS. Others worry about fraud in the home care setting. Still others worry about elder abuse (Schmitt, 2015).

Greater accountability will mean more costs for agencies. Even unions have entered the fray. While heavily represented in institutional settings, they are not nearly as strong with respect to home care workers who suffer low wages, poor working conditions, and poor benefits, as will be described below. Unionization would, of course, add to the financial worries of home care agencies who have resisted efforts to improve the wages and working conditions of PCAs.

There are still other forces that serve to stymie HCBS efforts. Most analysts predicted that HCBS would reduce hospitalizations and acute care costs. Contrary to expectations, however, there is no evidence as yet that this will be the case and studies have reported increased hospitalizations in home care as compared to nursing homes (Wysocki, 2014). While the reasons for this are not entirely clear, it is possible that nursing home RNs are able to identify and address medical issues before they require hospital-ization and are more aware of existing or emerging co-morbidities. Family caregivers and PCAs are probably less able to identify emerging co-morbid situations and more likely to call for emergency services.

If Medicaid continues to operate in the straitjacket created by state budget shortfalls and the need for cost controls, such forces will serve to stymie HCBS program growth and compromise quality.

Home care staff pay and working conditions

Chapter Four described the direct care staffing deficiencies in nursing homes: low pay, poor working conditions, and heavy workload. Burnout and injuries are endemic and turnover is high. The situation is even worse in the home care setting. PCAs and HHAs are paid even less, on aver-age, and have fewer benefits than the CNAs that staff nursing homes. They also have an even higher rate of injury due largely to the lack of available assistance and technology in the home care setting. Heavy lifting must often be done alone. (McCaughey et al., 2012).

According to the National Employment Law Project (Connolly, 2015), using data from AARP, PHI, and other organizations, home care workers suffer:

- *Poverty wages*: average annual earnings in 2014 were $18,598, qualifying most workers for welfare benefits including food stamps, housing subsidies, and childcare services.
- *Poor employee benefits*: most lack employer health insurance, paid time off, and paid sick time, although the ACA has mitigated the health insurance limitations.
- *Falling wages*: Over the last ten years, inflation adjusted wages have dropped 6%, with average hourly pay in 2014 at $10.30.
- *Unpredictable schedules*: Nearly half of home care workers do not have full-time or consistent work.

The Bureau of Labor Statistics reports similar wage data. According to their occupational surveys, real wages declined by 4.9% between 2002 and 2012 while growth in the PCA labor force grew by 96%, a remarkable disparity (Figures 7 and 8).

Figure 7. Personal care aide:
Rising numbers
2002–2012.

Figure 8. Personal care aide:
Falling wages
2002–2012.

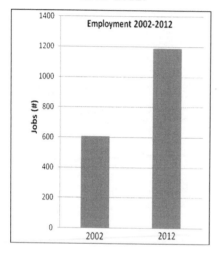

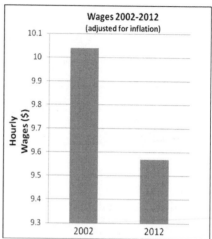

Source: Bureau of Labor Statistics

Source: Bureau of Labor Statistics

According to the 2015 Private Duty Benchmarking Survey, performed on behalf of the industry, more than 60% of aides working for private home care companies quit or were fired in 2014. The median turnover rate of 61.6% was the highest since the survey began in 2010, with agencies in the bottom quartile at over 100% turnover. The same survey found that 62% of home care agency administrators saw caregiver shortages as one of the greatest threats to the industry, up from 50% in 2013 (Home Care Pulse, 2015).

Staffing problems create poor home care quality

HCBS services are expanding rapidly, with minimal regard for quality of care. To receive a waiver, a state plan must provide assurances that each client will have a care plan and be treated by qualified staff, as defined by the states. States must also assure that they have a system in place that can monitor care and correct deficiencies. In 2003, however, the U.S. Government Accountability Office found that 70% of the programs it reviewed had problems with quality of care, including failure to provide necessary services, weaknesses in service plans, and inadequate case management (Government Accountability Office, 2003).

In 2012, the Office of Inspector General of the U.S. Health and Human Services Department inspected 25 state waiver programs and found that seven had failed to meet the terms of their quality assurances and that three of those had continued the failure up to the point of program renewal. Although the three programs were renewed, they still had not corrected deficiencies, well beyond the point of renewal. The Inspector General also found that CMS failed to adequately use its available tools to force corrective action (Levinson, 2012).

The federal government does not regulate the home care industry, relying on states to develop and enforce standards. Yet state regulations are light and enforcement is weak. Most states rely on the industry to self-regulate and generally conduct inspections only in response to complaints. Issues concerning the quality of home care staffing are not adequately addressed in this environment, including:

Poor Training: Most states have requirements for HHAs, who have responsibility for active medical care. However, with a few exceptions, they have essentially no requirements for PCAs. With some exceptions, states rely on the agencies themselves to define and provide orientation and training for PCAs, with most providing little or none. According to a 2014 study, only seven states had training requirements for PCAs that met at least one of four standards of rigor: specified training hours; a state exam; state-specified detailed competencies; a state sponsored curriculum (Marquand & Chapman, 2014).

Absenteeism and turnover: Consistency is a critical factor in high quality care. Disabled older adults get attached to a competent aide and may become frustrated when that aide must be absent for personal reasons. The new aide may not know the elder's needs and interests and be unable to meet expectations. Such absences are common because 90% of PCAs are women who often have assumed responsibility for children or their own parents. The high turnover rate magnifies this effect and it is not uncommon for an agency to send over 3–4 new aides before they find one who is compatible with the client, only to have the new aide leave after a few weeks or months, usually due to low pay, personal obstacles, or burnout.

Poor communication skills: Caring for a severely disabled older adult, particularly if dementia is involved, is difficult even for an aide with years of experience and good communication skills. It is sometimes simply impossible for aides with limited education, limited English-language skills, or a lack of awareness of the cultural background of the client. Twenty-five percent of PCAs are recent immigrants and such limitations can create communication breakdown and cause frustration on the part of the client (Kelly, Morgan, & Jason, 2013). In addition, 25% of PCAs lack a high school diploma, be it from the U.S. or another country, and have poor literacy skills (Kelly, Morgan, & Jason, 2013). Poor reading, writing, and numeracy skills can lead to errors and misunderstandings. Even such minor things as being unable to follow written instructions or find an unfamiliar program in a TV guide can lead to poor relations with a client.

Error, fraud, and abuse: The majority of home care agencies do not have on-site supervision of personal care assistants and those that have some supervision conduct only intermittent and occasional visits (Graham, 2013). This can allow for problems, including errors, fraud, and abuse. Aides may arrive late, leave during the day, or depart early while covering their tracks with the agency. Medications can be missed. Care needs can go unmet. Elders can be verbally and physically abused. Since home care sites are isolated and the very old are often unaware of what is going on around them, such abuse cannot be easily discovered. While the vast majority of home care workers are hardworking and dedicated, oversight is needed to help deter abuse.

Abuse can also work in reverse. Disabled older adults, particularly those suffering from dementia, frequently abuse caregivers without cause. They can do so directly through verbal and physical assault, or indirectly, by complaining to family members about their perceived abuse. It is difficult for family members to figure out what is actually happening and agencies must often wait for repeat complaints to distinguish incompetence in caregiving from an incorrect perception on the part of the client.

PACE: An effective model for home and community-based care

Given the complex nature of mental and physical health in the oldest old, failure to effectively coordinate care can lead to poor outcomes and dissatisfaction with care. Many of the weaknesses in Medicaid HCBS can be overcome by transcending the isolation of the individual residence, emphasizing community, and providing a comprehensive and holistic approach to care management. Such an approach is at the heart of the Program for All-Inclusive Care for the Elderly, or PACE. PACE integrates Medicare and Medicaid and deals comprehensively with the entire continuum of care and all relevant services, including medical, social services, and personal care. PACE providers across all services have access to the full history and current status of the client and can reach consensus decisions as to the best course of action in constantly changing health circumstances.

Care coordination and the PACE model

In the 1970s a non-profit group in the San Francisco area built a comprehensive long-term care program for members of the local immigrant community eligible for nursing home level care, mostly from Asia. Using a model based on the British day hospital, all housing, social, and medical services were combined into a single program aimed at keeping its participants in the community. The program eventually gained Medicaid eligibility and was expanded to include an adult day center and home delivery of meals.

In the 1980s, the program was given a grant by the U.S. Department of Health and Human Services to develop a consolidated model of care and to test a financing approach involving fixed per capita payments covering both medical and custodial care. In 1990, the federal government officially adopted this LTC approach as the Program for All-inclusive Care for the Elderly (PACE) and allowed 10 additional non-profit organizations to join the new financing system based on waivers from both Medicaid and Medicare. By the year 2000, there were 30 PACE programs operating nationally and the Balanced Budget Act of 1997 made PACE a permanently recognized provider type under both Medicaid and Medicare. By 2000, there were 30 programs operational in the U.S. As of 2015, there are 114 active programs in 32 states, with 26,000 participants (National PACE Association, 2015a).

PACE is based on the belief that it is better for the well-being of older adults with chronic care needs and their families to be served in the community whenever possible. PACE advocates that care is best provided comprehensively and holistically. By delivering all needed medical and supportive services, a PACE program is able to provide the entire continuum of care and services to those with chronic care needs while maintaining their independence in the home for as long as possible. Services include (National PACE Association, 2015a):

- adult day care that offers nursing, meals, nutritional counseling, social work, and ; physical, occupational, and recreational therapies;
- medical care provided by a PACE physician familiar with the history, needs, and preferences of each participant;
- home health care and personal care;
- all prescription drugs;
- social services;
- medical specialties, such as audiology, dentistry, optometry, podiatry, and speech therapy;
- respite care; and
- hospital and nursing home care, when necessary.

According to the National PACE Association (2015b), the typical PACE enrollee is 80 years old, has 7.9 medical conditions, and needs help with about three ADLs. Forty-nine percent have been diagnosed with dementia. Ninety percent live in the community.

PACE is intended to serve the local community and includes an inter-disciplinary care team under the direction of a PACE program manager. The team consists of a primary care physician, RN, social worker, physical therapist, pharmacist, occupational therapist, recreational therapist, dietitian, home-care coordinator, PCAs, and drivers. Medical and social services are offered centrally, at an adult day center that forms the hub of the program and provides a place where participants can socialize with others. Participants visit the center several days each week with the number of visits determined by need and level of disability. PACE arranges transportation (Center for Medicare Education, 2001).

PACE program outcomes

While individual PACE programs can vary in outcomes due, in part, to the length of time the program has been in existence and the effectiveness of program leadership, studies of PACE programs have consistently reported positive outcomes. The National Registry of Evidence-based Programs and Practices of the Substance Abuse and Mental Health Services Administration (2014) provides a summary of a number of these outcomes. In particular:

Aging in place: PACE enrollees unanimously prefer to live out their lives in their communities and the programs have proved successful in accomplishing this central programmatic goal. Although PACE continues to provide services even if a participant must enter a nursing home, studies have shown a lower rate of nursing home admissions (Chatterji, Burstein,

Kidder, & White, 1998). A 2002 study reported that only 24% of PACE enrollees died in hospitals compared to 53% of traditional Medicare beneficiaries, a significant difference. The same study found that PACE enrollees were more than twice as likely to die at home as compared to the general older population (Temkin-Greener & Mukamel, 2002).

Quality of care: Delivery of care holistically and comprehensively provides many ways to improve the quality of care. Medications are better managed, preventive care is emphasized (Beauchamp, Cheh, Schmitz, Kemper, & Hall, 2008), and new or changed conditions can be dealt with more quickly. Many studies point to both improved outcomes and a greater level of satisfaction by participants and their families (Mitchell, Polivka, & Wang, 2008). Participants reported more contact with providers (Kane, Homyak, Bershadsky, & Flood, 2006) and relative ease of accessing care (Beauchamp et al., 2008). In addition, research has shown that the PACE program has significantly lower turnover rate for PCAs. A rate of only 12% was reported in the Institute of Medicine's 2008 report on the healthcare workforce (Institute of Medicine, 2008)

Hospital and ER visits: A major barrier to the goal of aging in place is difficulty in addressing changes in chronic conditions, new conditions, and medical emergencies. These are more easily managed in nursing homes, particularly those associated with hospitals. Studies have shown, however, that PACE program participants were less likely to be hospitalized (Beauchamp et al., 2008) and spent less time in an average hospital stay (Mitchell et al., 2008). One study found that reduced levels of hospitalizations occurred because PACE reduced the level of unmet need (Sands et al., 2006).

Quality of life: In addition to improved quality of care, participants and their families reported improved quality of life and mental health in the PACE environment. There was less depression and worry (Beauchamp et al., 2008) and greater attendance at social activities (Chatterji et al., 1998).

PACE costs

Although cost has not been a priority consideration in the course of care, the program received federal authorization on the expectation that maintaining older adults in the community with PACE comprehensive care would be no more costly than other HCBS programs, both fee for service and fixed sum per capita. Since HCBS waiver program costs vary from state to state, and Medicaid reimbursement rates also vary, such a comparison is difficult to make. In addition, some of the major outcomes for PACE, participant and family satisfaction, for example, are difficult to quantify in terms of cost. Mortality rates are also a difficult metric to use for comparison since longer life can potentially mean more costs.

A 2014 review commissioned by the U.S. Health and Human Services Department found mixed results with respect to Medicaid and Medicare costs. The study compared PACE costs with the estimated costs for an alternate enrollment in an HCBS waiver program. Seven of the eight states studied showed higher PACE costs, due primarily to the Medicaid component, but with a closing of the gap several years after enrollment. New York was the exception where costs were found to be generally comparable from the outset. The study concluded by suggesting that policy makers would ultimately have to base the value of the PACE program on factors other than costs, including quality of care, satisfaction levels, and health outcomes (Ghosh, Schmitz, & Brown, 2014).

The importance of the PACE paradigm

PACE provides a viable model for the management of community-based long-term care by bringing medical and personal care aspects together in one program. The breadth and depth of care coordination can overcome many of the inherent concerns that accompany in-home care. The model can potentially:

- Overcome the social isolation of living alone at a very old age.
- Allow for the integration of home health with personal care, making the "advanced" personal care assistant more feasible by providing increased supervision of personal care activity.
- Monitor health status on a weekly basis and pursue treatment changes and acute care in a timely manner.
- Facilitate the effective delivery of preventative services.
- Enhance communication among providers through a common database and medical history profile.
- Increase the delivery of nutritional counseling and physical/occupational therapy through the adult day center.
- Reduce PCA turnover and improve communication between the PCA and other providers.
- More effectively manage transitions into and out of hospitals and rehabilitation facilities.

This level of care coordination and management, if feasible on a national level, would be ideal for a new long-term care insurance program. However, there are formidable obstacles to developing this approach on the scale needed over the next several decades.

PACE limitations

According to the U.S. Health and Human Services Department's National Registry of Evidence-based Programs and Practices (2014), there were only 26,000 participants in PACE programs nationally as of 2013. This represents less than 1% of those eligible for a PACE program. Given the intense interest in community-based LTC services and significant bipartisan support in Congress and the states, this would indicate that the program faces significant barriers to expansion. They include:

Cost of entry: Start-up costs for a PACE program are high, due mostly to the need to design, build, and staff a community adult day center that can provide both medical and social services to seriously disabled older adults. Non-profit organizations do not usually have the capital resources to build such a center. Demonstration projects received funds from foundations and other sources, but such money is less available now that the initial phase is over. The federal government has opened up the PACE program to for-profit organizations, but few seem interested. They do not want to risk heavy start-up costs if Medicaid and Medicare reimbursement and capitation levels are under pressure, and the program is generally too expensive for private payers (Lynch, 2008).

Some features are not acceptable to potential enrollees: PACE requires the use of PACE doctors and other professionals. Some potential enrollees prefer to stay with their own providers. Program modifications that allow for this are under consideration. Resistance also comes from those who do not like the idea of traveling frequently to a day center. This is particularly the case in rural areas where trips could be quite lengthy (Lynch, 2008).

Uncertain market: Making the upfront investment requires some certainty about the extent of the local market. This may be difficult if the PACE center competes with other options, including nursing homes. Non-profits lack the financial resources for conducting sustained marketing and outreach. They also lack the cushion that could be provided by private pay clients (Lynch, 2008).

State budgets: As with all community LTC options, constraints on state budgets make both the upfront investment and the sustainability of a program uncertain. This includes concerns about increased Medicaid costs resulting from individuals, who would not have otherwise pursued Medicaid, seeking to become Medicaid-eligible in order to join a PACE community (Lynch, 2008).

Can PACE and Medicaid HCBS mitigate the 2030 crisis?

Despite its value, PACE will not be able to meet the long-term need. Built to serve the Medicaid-eligible poor, increasing participation to become part of a broader long-term care program would be difficult. Building and staffing tens of thousands of adult day centers, locality by locality, would be fraught with financial, logistical, and political difficulties. It would no doubt require a huge infusion of federal funding. Yet, funds are desperately needed for improving nursing homes and upgrading the PCA workforce.

It will be quite difficult to address the impending caregiver crisis with Medicaid, which was intended to serve very sick indigent elders, disabled younger adults, and the poor. Medicaid cannot shirk this mandate and must therefore be judicious in how it provides services to aging boomers who would otherwise have no way to pay for care. Disabled boomers in need will be faced with having to cash in assets and "spend down" a lifetime of savings to access care that years of contributions to social security and Medicare do not cover. They will spend money they had put aside to make retirement a positive experience or to pass along to children.

They will also only be able to access a level of care that a state can afford, as determined by state governments and the taxpayers who would need to fund any increase in social services. As currently constituted, and under state budget constraints and an ethos that opposes increased welfare spending, qualifying for such care would be problematic at best. Nearly all states are already embracing a wide range of cost cutting or containment strategies.

Perhaps the most insidious cost-cutting strategy is switching from fee-for-service reimbursement for home care to capitated managed care options. Such programs would provide only a fixed amount of reimbursement per client in certain categories, in an effort to encourage more cost-effective practices in home care agencies. Given the track record of private agencies and the lack of accountability in the diffuse settings of home care, quality will likely be compromised by this strategy. The only question would be: compromised by how much?

There are already major deficiencies in the U.S. long-term care system, in both nursing homes and the community, including a shortage of professional services, high rates of burn-out and turnover in the direct care workforce, poor quality control systems, and failure to meet the expectations of older adults and their families for a more person-centered care. Financial constraints will worsen an already burdened system.

Family caregivers can only benefit if personal care services, assistive technology, or case management is provided. Such services could delay or avoid nursing home placement in a number of cases. Yet, the dilemma will always be there. If quality is perceived to be poor, older adults and their families will not be willing to cash in or spend down assets to access care. Some older adults will simply live alone under increasingly dangerous circumstances. Some caregivers will take on even greater burden, at the expense of their livelihoods and health. If quality is perceived to be good, on the other hand, people will come "out of the woodwork" to increase demand for services that states and taxpayers are unprepared to fund.

The next chapter looks at policy options that recognize this dilemma and take a more expansive approach to addressing it.

Chapter Eight

Addressing the 2030 crisis: Expand Medicare to fund an army of personal care assistants

Long-term personal care in the U.S. is heavily dependent on unpaid family caregiving. It is worth repeating that at least 90% of older persons receiving help with ADLs received some informal care in 2011 and about two-thirds received only informal care. Family caregivers in non-institutional settings collectively provided 75–80% of total care hours (Spillman et al., 2014).

The projection of a 2030 crisis is based on demographic trends that cannot be changed, a dramatic rise in the number of older adults needing daily care and an equally dramatic decline of available family caregivers. In addition, optimism about future boomer health and financial status appears unwarranted, and economic prospects for boomer children are not good.

Family caregiving is the very essence of the person-centered care being promoted by advocates for aging in place. With an impending sharp decline in caregivers and with the need for those caregivers to stay in the workplace in order to support their own families, delivery of in-home, person-centered care must inevitably default to the use of personal care services, i.e., PCAs.

Given the anticipated dramatic growth in the prevalence of conditions like dementia, which require high-intensity care, aging boomers will need, in effect, an army of PCAs. These aides will be required in all care settings and across all social classes. Disability in old age knows no boundaries.

This chapter describes what recruiting and deploying such an army might look like. It argues for creating a national universal long-term care insurance program, a new "Part" of Medicare, in effect, to fund this army. Medicare was created when the overwhelming majority of citizens saw that providing medical help to the aged was in the best interest of society at large. The program later expanded to include mental health parity, prescription drugs, and hospice care. It is now time to add long-term personal care. The following are the essential elements of a comprehensive approach to expanding personal care services in all settings:

- Add long-term care services to Medicare to fund personal care assistance in all settings and care coordination in the community.
- Include family caregivers in any paid system.
- Expand the PCA workforce and improve training, compensation, and working conditions.
- Build a cadre of certified advanced PCAs capable of carrying out basic medical tasks and helping with care coordination.
- Make round-the-clock care the standard for older adults living at home with severe disability and/or moderate to advanced dementia.

- Require nursing homes to provide private rooms to all residents and employ PCAs to bolster direct care staffing and provide resident-centered care.

- Require all nursing homes to have dementia SCUs and provide specialized dementia training for PCAs working in nursing homes, assisted living facilities, and private residences.

- Add geriatrics to all medical and nursing school curriculum areas and provide incentives to increase the supply of geriatricians, geriatric nurses, geriatric social workers, and geriatric mental health professionals.

Toward a universal long-term personal care benefit

Many designs have been put forward for a Medicare-like public LTC insurance program. Since the collapse of the voluntary CLASS program associated with the Affordable Care Act, new proposals have usually involved mandatory insurance to avoid adverse selection. They have varied primarily in funding strategy.

Funding approaches have looked at various types of taxation, including increased Medicare and/or Social Security taxes, and at added premiums (Folbre & Wolf, 2012). Most proposals are structured to require more from those with greater wealth, including various types of asset spend-downs (Folbre & Wolf, 2012). Some look to public-private partnerships such as a private marketplace for long-term services, or a core LTC benefit supplemented by private insurance to cover gaps caused by more expensive services. Deductibles and co-pays of various sorts have been proposed to control cost and limit non-essential use of some services. Some call for a significant buy-in, amounting to perhaps the cost of six months of equivalent nursing home care, before the program kicks in (Folbre & Wolf, 2012).

The details of a new universal public long-term care insurance benefit would need to be worked out by the government and appropriate technical experts. Several efforts are underway, including the work of the Long-Term Care Financing Collaborative that has brought together technical experts and both public and private stakeholders. The collaborative includes representatives of a wide variety of political viewpoints (Long-Term Care Financing Collaborative, 2015). There are several important elements, however, that should be part of any new program:

Universality: To avoid adverse selection, the program must be mandatory for all those over a set age and spread risk as widely as possible. It should cover anyone with a disability level that would qualify for Medicaid nursing home admission.

Flexible eligibility requirements: While a fixed standard can be established for program access, e.g., assistance with two or more ADLs, the program must allow for significant use of professional judgment for cases that cannot be easily quantified, including consideration of the client's mental capacity and psychological co-morbidities. Any appeal process must be transparent and timely.

Comprehensive benefits: The program must include all reasonable and necessary services for those needing help, including skilled institutional or home nursing, home health aide services, personal care services, care management and coordination, adult day care, family caregiver respite, transportation, and outpatient therapies. Individuals may respond differently to different kinds of services and the program should consider client preferences.

Personal care services: Eligible participants must be entitled to up to round-the-clock paid personal care with ADLs in the home, assisted living facility, or other community setting. This can include paid formal help as well as meaningful compensation for family caregivers through wages and/ or tax benefits. Nursing home residents would also be entitled to enough one-to-one paid personal care to cover any need for personal care services caused by high CNA resident caseloads.

Coordination of care: The program must support an effective care management process in the community. A recipient needs someone to direct personal care workers, manage relevant instrumental activities of daily living (IADLs), and interact with medical and social services personnel. This should be the client, if competent, or a family member or friend. If neither is available, a non-profit agency or social worker should be assigned, at public expense. Information and telecommunications technology should become integrated into care coordination to facilitate communication and inform decision-making.

Quality control: States must be required to certify care providers for the program and implement a program of regular follow-up to assure quality and safety. Workers at all levels must be trained and certified according to nationally-defined standards.

Reimbursement levels: Reimbursement must be set at levels that can assure quality. This must include compensation levels for PCAs and home health aides that provide a living wage based upon the prevailing cost of living in the area of service, along with benefits. Working conditions must be conducive to effective care.

The role of family caregiving

A universal LTC public insurance program would be of clear benefit to disabled elders without available family resources. A major concern expressed by those looking for a cost-effective way to provide such a benefit, however, is the possibility of runaway expenses caused by a rapid and steep decline in informal care. Caregivers will want to stay in the workforce and limit the extent of caregiving as much as possible.

While family members may want to limit caregiving, they still see it as part of their moral responsibility and want to be a part of the caregiving process. Part of the rationale for paying family caregivers is to provide at least some way for a family member to engage in caregiving without making a large financial sacrifice.

In addition, a reduction in family caregiving would be a good thing in and of itself, for the caregiver, her family, her community, and, indeed, the national economy should the family member remain productively employed. Family caregivers would be healthier and happier with corresponding reductions in their use of the medical and mental health services needed to treat the many stress-related conditions that stem from excess burden.

The goal of any new LTC program would be to get the family caregiver either out of the business of tending to ADLs, or to pay them for the work. This would allow the family member to engage, unpaid, with the many needed IADLs, including shopping, banking, travel, and coordination with caregivers and medical providers. The family member will also have more time to provide the kind of companionship that only a friend or family member can provide.

There will undoubtedly be some woodwork effects, an evitable consequence of the presence of unmet need and unsustainable caregiver burden. When Medicare itself was started, there was an initial uptick in activity and cost as unmet need was unshackled. The same was true when new benefits were added. But the program eventually settled onto a generally sound actuarial footing. Low administrative costs, significant economies of scale, and careful setting of reimbursement rates balanced the effect of increased use (Moon, 2015).

A new Medicare LTC benefit will likely go through a similar uptick and, like other new Medicare programs, will eventually settle into a balance between costs and burdens. If this balance is achieved, the oldest old and their families will have sufficient LTC options with which to face the upcoming crisis.

Paid family caregivers

Providing compensation for caregiving by family members and friends has been discussed widely. Many states have developed Medicaid or VA programs based on so-called consumer-directed care, which allows for such compensation.

Medicaid consumer-directed care

A majority of states have Medicaid waivers that allow participants to receive care at home instead of in a nursing home and to direct their own care. In such "cash and counseling" programs, participants are free to select care providers and can employ adult children, other relatives, or friends (Robert Wood Johnson Foundation, 2015c). Some states even allow for paying spouses. Older adults must be considered employers and family caregivers would be employees. Both would assume responsibility for paying appropriate taxes.

Half the states include personal care services in their state Medicaid plans. Some of these programs also allow for consumer direction of care, enabling participants to hire friends and family members. As noted earlier, however, there are usually typically caps to Medicaid PCS plans and they allow for very few hours of care (Kaiser Family Foundation, 2012). Eligibility requirements are also much more stringent than those of waiver programs (Ng, Harrington, Musuneci, & Reaves, 2014).

Medicaid life settlements

Medicaid life settlements, also known as "life care funding plans", are for holders of life insurance policies who are considering Medicaid for long-term care (American Elder Care Research Organization, 2015). Life insurance policies are normally considered assets which may disqualify a holder from Medicaid eligibility, but this program allows the individual to convert the policy into a dollar amount of care services. The money is put into an account and used to pay for care for the policyholder. It can be used for any type of care, including home care and assisted living, and home modifications that help older adults maintain their independence. It can also be used to pay family members for the care they provide, at the Medicaid rate (American Eldercare Research Organization, 2015).

The account is considered a Medicaid-qualified spend down, allowing care to start before assets are fully exhausted. When the fund is depleted the individual is likely to qualify for Medicaid.

Indirect forms of compensation

Some indirect caregiving compensation comes through IRS and state tax rules. Disabled parents or other relatives may qualify as dependents if more than half their living costs are paid by a family member, or by more than one family member collectively (Bell, 2015). Even if not so qualified, deductions can be declared if the relative pays some medical expenses or gives up a portion of her home. If caring for an elder is needed in order for a spouse or other relative to be able to work, there may also be eligibility for a tax credit (Bell, 2015).

Effectiveness of consumer-directed programs

Consumer-directed programs that allow family members to be paid as caregivers have been viewed favorably by older adults and their families, and are growing. A review of programs in fifteen states, found that, although somewhat more expensive than agency-directed services, such programs reduce unmet need and improve care quality and health outcomes, which could serve to reduce costs in the long run. (Robert Wood Johnson Foundation, 2015b). An earlier review of pilot programs in three states found similar results (Carlson, Foster, Dale, & Brown, 2007).

In addition, fear of fraud has proved largely unfounded and studies indicate that if a written care plan is required and reviewed, and if proper oversight is maintained, the program can proceed with few instances of abuse (Schore, Foster, & Phillips, 2007; Simon-Rusinowitz, Loughlin, & Mahoney, 2011).

One area of concern, however, involves the competence of the older adult and the family caregiver. Since only nursing home-eligible patients can enter the program, participants are necessarily severely physically disabled or suffering from dementia. In addition, as noted earlier, many family caregivers find themselves providing complex medical care under poorly supervised conditions. While programs may provide advice to the older adult or her representative, those favoring the expansion of consumer-directed cash and counseling programs agree that caregivers must receive more training if care is to be administered safely Reinhard, Given, Petlick, & Bemis, 2008).

Offering compensation to family members and friends for managing ADLs and complex medical care makes sense in an LTC program that covers personal care assistance. It would reduce dependence on aides and allow family members and friends to enjoy the positive aspects of caring for a loved one.

More personal care assistants

We have discussed the role of direct care workers at length in both community and institutional settings. They must play a central role in future long-term care. As the extent of family caregiving declines, PCAs can fill the gap by providing added person-centered care. In addition to assisting with basic ADLs, they can provide companionship, help with preferred meals and snacks, and transfer, on demand, into and out of bed, chair, and wheelchair. They can keep the home care setting clean, comfortable, and safe. They can accompany the elder on visits to physicians, clinics, friends, family members, local parks, and shopping destinations. They can provide reminders for medication and physical therapy exercises, and help the older adult communicate with family members and service providers.

PCAs can do much to make life more interesting and bearable for an older adult.

Upgrading the direct care workforce

There is a shortage of direct care workers and the Bureau of Labor Statistics (BLS) is already projecting a massive, growing demand. In 2013, the BLS projected that personal care assistant will be the fastest growing occupation in the U.S. in the ten years between 2012 and 2022 (580,000 new positions). Home health aide is at number four (424,000 new jobs) and nurse aide at number six (312,000 new jobs) (Paraprofessional Healthcare Institute, 2014b).

Future projections may be underestimated, however, because they do not take fully into account the many aides hired directly by families in the so-called gray market. In addition, the demand numbers do not take into account the ongoing serious level of unmet need. As mentioned earlier, a 2014 U.S. Department of Health and Human Services research report indicated that one in three older adults needing help with two or more ADLs has an adverse consequence due to unmet need for assistance with ADLs within any given month (Freedman & Spillman, 2014). The BLS projections were also made only through 2022, a decade before the number of oldest old boomers starts to reach its peak. The shortage will grow worse by that time particularly if the incidence of disability increases.

The real and worsening current shortage of PCAs is due largely to poor pay and benefits, heavy workloads, injury, irregular hours, the inability to cope with clients, and poor communication skills. Burnout and turnover are not improving, yet the number of unfilled positions is already growing rapidly, putting even greater stress on the LTC system and forcing agencies to further reduce their already low hiring standards.

To attract and retain PCAs, they can no longer be treated as mere companions, but as true paraprofessionals. The very nature of the job must be changed in several critical ways:

Workforce status: As mentioned in Chapter Seven, the Obama administration declared in 2013 that, starting in 2015, personal care workers were to no longer be classified as companions, the equivalent of babysitters, and would become eligible for minimum wage, overtime, and other benefits as set by the Fair Labor Standards Act for non-exempt employees. A federal court, however, relying on prior legislation by Congress, overruled the Obama administration and indicated that only Congress could change the status of these workers. As expected, home care agencies, mostly for-profit companies, supported the court's action. The new status would potentially increase costs and cut into profits.

The U.S. Court of Appeals for the Washington, D.C. District reversed the lower court ruling in August 2015, confirming that the U.S. Department of Labor acted with proper authority in changing the classification of personal care workers based on the fact that they performed work that went beyond the scope of the original classification. Home care agencies are appealing the case, however, and implementing the new requirements will still be a challenge as agencies consider ways to get around the new ruling, including reducing work hours to avoid overtime. If some agencies are forced to shut down because they could not afford the added costs, this could create further problems.

Full-time salaries with benefits: PCAs must be paid a competitive wage and be considered full-time employees with a stable salary, health benefits, sick leave, and personal/vacation time. Family leave benefits are also a priority since many aides are also managing care for their own children or parents. Numerous studies have shown a correlation between low wages and lack of full-time status, and turnover (Barbarotta, 2010). These are also factors that probably keep new workers from entering the occupation.

Management practices and organizational culture: PCAs frequently complain about poor or insufficient supervision, lack of training and support, and poor job design. Scheduling, for example, is often arbitrary and without regard for employee circumstances. Many workers have other responsibilities and should be able to rely on a consistent schedule, to the extent possible, that changes only with sufficient advance notice (Connolly, 2015). In most cases, this kind of management failure is perceived as personal disrespect and fosters poor relationships between workers and supervisors. Such disrespect has been identified as another major reason for employee turnover (Barbarotta, 2010). When direct care workers are included in management teams, as in culture change initiatives, absenteeism diminishes and retention improves (Doty, Koren, & Sturla, 2008).

Career advancement: In addition to being among the lowest paid workers nationally, PCAs have virtually no path for career advancement, another major factor leading to turnover and impacting the ability to recruit new workers. With some thought, workers with more experience and training can assume roles that take advantage of their knowledge, such as mentors for newly hired workers, team leaders, and participants in care management teams. Incentives can be provided to agencies that improve advancement opportunities for PCAs.

More training: Although a few states have meaningful training standards for Medicaid-eligible PCAs, in most states such workers receive little or no training. There are model curricula for PCAs that have been tested and found effective, however. The 77-hour curriculum used by

Paraprofessional Healthcare Institute is illustrative and could be the basis for a national mandatory training program for PCAs (Paraprofessional Healthcare Institute, 2009). It includes:

- Introduction to the direct care setting
- Professionalism and teamwork
- Infection control
- Body mechanics
- Body systems and common diseases
- Working with elders
- Respecting differences
- Communication skills
- Supporting consumers safely at home
- Ambulating and making a bed
- Supporting consumer dignity while providing care
- Bathing and personal care
- Working with Alzheimer's Disease consumers
- Dressing and toileting
- Working with an independent adult with physical disabilities
- Eating
- Depression, mental illness, abuse and neglect
- Consumer and worker rights
- Managing time and managing stress

Studies have shown that increased training for PCAs improves care and patient and family satisfaction. It also reduces turnover and burn-out (Paraprofessional Healthcare Institute, 2005).

National recruitment campaign: Some have suggested that the federal government create a national program for recruiting direct care workers, including PCAs, home health aides and nurse aides. Others have suggested focused recruitment efforts through state and county workforce development centers to better match workers with conveniently located openings and to conduct orientation and training, as needed (Fishman, Barnow, Glosser, & Gardiner, 2004). Still others have suggested special programs to provide additional visas to encourage the immigration of potential long-term care workers, and legal status for undocumented immigrants serving in long-term care positions (Polson, 2011; Hess & Henrici, 2013). Engaging retired healthcare workers and others in part-time direct care work is another possibility (Stone, 2012).

Advanced personal care assistants

A consistent complaint about long-term care in the U.S. is the overlapping and confusing borders separating Medicaid and Medicare services. In addition to increased bureaucratic load and the associated frustrations, the disjointed nature of the system can increase costs and create obstacles to potential efficiencies (National Committee for Quality Assurance, 2013).

One such obstacle involves the separation of medical and personal care tasks (Eldercare Workforce Alliance, 2014). The current environment creates a number of awkward situations. We saw that unqualified family caregivers often provide medical care to their relatives. We also know that, in most states, PCAs can remind a care recipient to take her medications, but cannot put them into medication cups or directly administer them. Having little or no training, PCAs are also usually forbidden to carry out even very basic medical tasks, such as simple wound care, or taking temperature or pulse oximeter readings. Nurses and home health aides must be separately deployed to do these things, even for stable patients. In many cases, family members stop by to administer medications while PCAs just watch.

As community care becomes the prevailing paradigm, however, families and their aging relatives will benefit if PCAs take on more advanced tasks after receiving appropriate training, at the outset of employment or as circumstances dictate. If PCAs were given rudimentary training, of the sort currently received by many home health aides, for example, care could be delivered far more efficiently, with less need for expensive nursing care and perhaps fewer visits to emergency rooms. It would also allow for better coordination of care.

A relatively small upgrade in training protocol would create, in effect, a merging of the personal care assistant and home health aide job descriptions. This new position, advanced personal care assistant, could involve specific training and certification, and be required of any long-term care worker assigned under any federally-supported long-term care program. The Eldercare Workforce Alliance, a consortium of 31 organizations devoted to caregiving for older adults, issued a 2014 consensus policy brief calling for the development of an Advanced Direct Care Worker position for federal programs. It would be based on a training program aimed at providing the kind of skills that PCAs would need to efficiently fill caregiving gaps. Such advanced training would include (Eldercare Workforce Alliance, 2014):

- *Assistance with medical and nursing tasks*: This might include inserting, removing, and maintaining catheters, overseeing nebulizer treatments, administering enemas and suppositories, assisting with minor cuts, abrasions and wound care, taking readings and measurements, monitoring insulin levels, and supporting pain management. The advanced worker would also be more directly engaged in medication administration and monitoring. Workers could be trained to recognize common medical symptoms and drug side effects.

- *Providing health information and resources*: Personal care workers could be trained to provide direction to clients on basic nutrition and health promotion best practices, including the value of proper dental care and exercise. They could also help physical therapists by directing simple exercises as prescribed.

- *Care coordination*: The advanced personal care worker could play an important role in care coordination, helping service providers understand the client and communicating the care plan to the client and her family. Training in this area could include communication skills, cultural competency, and the ethics of patient care.

Community colleges, non-profit organizations, and community workforce development agencies could be brought into the training process. Some sort of federally directed or endorsed certification would also be important. It would affirm the value of the worker, make it easier to transfer between jobs and states, and ensure the integrity of federally-funded long-term care programs.

Who would be trained?

The Eldercare Workforce Alliance recommends launching demon-stration projects for this new position but does not make specific refer-ence to any new certification or recommendations as to how many PCAs should be trained in advanced skills. There are a number of possible ways to proceed. There could be some advanced training for all PCAs. There could also be a tiered training program, restricting advanced training to aides with significant experience, higher-level communication skills, and/ or stronger educational backgrounds. Workers who care for disabled older adults with no involvement of family members should clearly be a priority for training in at least some advanced skills.

The development of an advanced position would also help retention by providing a career path for PCAs with, presumably, enhanced compen-sation. Certification would also enhance the professional standing of aides and their ability to command respect from supervisors and other health-care workers.

Round-the-clock personal care in the community

In 2013, Medicaid reached a turning point. More dollars are now spent on community care than on nursing homes, symbolizing the strong surge of public interest in the aging-in-place approach to LTC, and the trend is likely to continue (Eiken, Sredl, Burwell, & Saucier, 2015). Yet, Medicaid community personal care services are paltry, as described in Chapter Seven. They are intended to supplement family caregiving with, at best, a few hours per day of assistance. Those without family caregivers will therefore have no choice but to either live mostly alone, at high risk of injury, untreated illness, or death, or enter a facility.

Nursing homes provide round-the-clock care for disabled elders and safety is of paramount importance. This represents a serious disconnect. If an older adult is considered ready for nursing home care, why would it be acceptable to leave them in their homes with aides looking in on them for just a few hours a day? Short of living with a relative, elders would have no one to help during the night or in the early morning hours when many are awake, possibly hungry, and potentially active. If incontinence is an issue, and it affects over half of those in nursing homes (Leung & Schnelle, 2008), is it acceptable to leave an older adult soaking in an adult diaper at home until an aide arrives many hours later?

Not all disabled older adults need round-the-clock care. However, 12+ hours of care should be a minimum, spanning the time from wake-up to dinner, and we should make round-the-clock combined formal and informal care available to all, based upon professional recommendation. Using nursing home care as a reference point, the true daily need for an older adult living alone and suffering from moderate to severe dementia and/or limitations with two or more ADLs is round-the-clock care. It is the only way to ensure safety and meet the full cycle of daily care needs in a person-centered manner.

An example: Older adult falls

While there are many ways in which home care can be inadequate, the risk of falls is probably of the greatest consequence. According to the CDC (2015a), falls are the leading cause of both fatal and non-fatal injuries in older adults. In 2013, 2.5 million falls among older adults were treated in emergency departments with 734,000 being hospitalized, numbers up substantially from a decade earlier. Those who have been injured from a fall also have an increased likelihood of experiencing additional falls. The direct medical cost of falls, adjusted for inflation, was $34 billion in 2013 (CDC, 2015b).

In addition to causing the fractures and traumatic brain injuries that may compromise independent living, falls can also cause an obsessive fear of falling that can limit physical activity and contribute to increasing frailty and weakness (CDC, 2015a).

Falls occur in nursing homes despite intense attention paid to preventing them. As more older adults live alone in the community, or with insufficient hours of care, falls could increase significantly over the coming decades and become a major concern for the aging-in-place movement. Round-the-clock personal care can play a significant role in preventing falls and reducing fall-related hospitalizations.

An example: Dementia

According to the Alzheimer's Association, one in seven Alzheimer's patients lives alone and half of those do not have a designated caregiver. If other dementias are included, the number may be as many as one million living alone (Alzheimer's Association, 2012). As substantial as these numbers are, however, they underestimate the problem as they do not include cases that are undiagnosed (Alzheimer's Association, 2012). The dangers of living alone with dementia include (Spencer, 2013):

- Those who smoke or try to cook can inadvertently cause gas leaks and fires. They may also have trouble calling for emergency services in the event of a fire, spreading the risk to neighboring homes.

- An estimated 60% of Alzheimer's patients will wander and get lost even in familiar places, exposing them to potential hazards including those associated with weather (see also Alzheimer's Association, 2015). Some may confuse day and night and start wandering inside and outside the house, further increasing risk.

- Dementia patients may get injured attempting familiar and unfamiliar tasks and hobbies that use tools, appliances, and equipment.

- Dementia patients may have trouble managing medications, alcohol consumption, and household toxins, creating risk for overdose and poisoning.

- Dementia patients may open the door to strangers, give away possessions to random people, and fall for phone solicitations and outright scams. They may use credit cards to make inappropriate purchases.

- Dementia patients are easily confused and may not know how to get help in a problematic situation. They may fail to use medical-alert systems even after receiving instruction in their use.

- Dementia confusion can easily lead to falls, even in individuals who have no problem walking.

It is, of course, difficult to know when round-the-clock care is needed for older adults with dementia. When boomers become the oldest old and suffer from dementia in staggering numbers, the drive to keep older adults in their homes for as long as possible without fully attentive care could contribute to further disability and caregiver worry.

There are other reasons why intensive home care is essential. Older disabled adults can suffer from social isolation when living alone which has been shown to contribute to mental health issues which can, in turn, affect general health (Dean, Kolody, Wood, & Matt, 1992). Depressed and lonely elders can also suffer from poor nutrition if they cannot manage shopping and meal preparation, or lose interest. Kitchens and bathrooms can become unclean and sources of infection. Poor eyesight or hearing can compromise many aspects of daily functioning.

Limits to round-the-clock care in the community

Not all older adults can be cared for round-the-clock in the community and advocates for aging in place are sometimes overly optimistic about who can receive care. Patients with advanced dementia, behavioral problems, complex chronic conditions, and multiple disabilities may prove to be impossible to maintain in the community even with full-time family caregiving. In New York City, Medicaid will pay for round-the-clock personal care through its Home Attendant II program, both live-in and fully awake double shifts, but only under specific conditions (New York State Department of Health, 2013):

- It is certified as necessary, due to extensive disability (needing help with 2 or more ADLs), by a physician.
- The recipient is medically stable and can be safely managed at home.
- The recipient, or a family member or friend living close by, can direct care through interaction with the PCA, supervisors, physicians, and others, and who can manage medications, physician visits, and other instrumental needs.

Careful consideration must be given to the feasibility of round-the-clock home care, on a case-by-case basis.

Private rooms and employing PCAs in nursing homes

Nursing homes should not have to compete for public resources with home and community-based services. All forms of services will be needed when boomers become the oldest old. However, nursing homes must become more attractive settings. They must offer more person-centered care and address the emotional needs of residents and their families.

While small homes, based on Green House principles, appear able to accomplish these objectives, formidable upfront costs and geographical limitations indicate that small homes will fill, at most, a fraction of the need. A more practical approach would be to treat a traditional nursing home more like a residence. This can be done without a hearth. It would require providing all residents with private rooms and providing PCAs to supplement CNAs and attend to resident interests and needs.

Private rooms

Nursing homes were originally constructed using a hospital model. They provide semi-private rooms for most and private rooms for some. Semi-private rooms, where residents are separated by a curtain and share a restroom, may work for short-term hospital stays, or perhaps 30-day rehabilitation stints, but they are not conducive to delivering long-term person-centered care. Family members looking to provide assistance are difficult to physically accommodate, there is little privacy, and room-mates are often incompatible, especially if one or both exhibit behavioral problems.

A private room can more easily accommodate a family member and, most importantly, could accommodate a PCA for some daytime hours. A private room with an easy chair, bathroom, small refrigerator, microwave, TV, internet connection, and phone would provide an environment in which caregiving can be managed comfortably. The room could be decorated according to the resident's taste.

Nursing homes will not be able to truly relieve family caregiver burden unless the caregiver knows that her loved one is being treated like a person, not a patient. Nursing homes must convert most semi-private rooms to private rooms, or build facility extensions with private rooms.

Employing PCAs in nursing homes

The central issue facing nursing homes is the shortage of professional and direct care staff. Without sufficient direct care staff residents are left with unmet need and can become emotionally distressed. This attitude is then expressed to families, who experience their own distress and communicate their concerns to staff members. Overburdened CNAs are unable to deliver the person-centered care that culture change reform asks of them.

What residents really need is additional basic personal care. If the resident wakes up especially early, for example, they need someone to attend to their toileting and dressing at that time, not two hours later, and perhaps provide breakfast. The resident may also need help with little things like finding a favorite TV show, transferring to a chair, taking a walk in the garden, getting a snack, visiting the facility library, or telephoning a family member.

These are tasks that can be carried out by a PCA, leaving the CNA to deal with her other responsibilities. The presence of PCAs would allow for flexible, resident-directed scheduling, an important part of culture change and person-centered care. It avoids the embarrassing practice of lining hallways or community rooms with frustrated and embittered wheel-chair-bound residents, often for hours, as they wait for mealtime or some other activity. This current, much-hated practice is caused by the require-ment that residents not be left alone in their rooms in an ambulatory state.

Using PCAs in nursing homes would be largely unprecedented and timing and protocol would have to be worked out. Depending on the type and severity of disability, the aide might be needed for only a few hours or for perhaps as many as 12 hours. They should not be needed during evening and night hours. Under any circumstances, however, this would be a more cost-effective way to solve the staffing shortage than hiring and training additional CNAs, at greater expense, to reduce caseloads. At the same time, hiring PCAs would provide residents with timely assistance in accordance with their own wishes and help reduce the current pervasive sterility and negativity that stigmatizes the industry.

If PCAs were to be effectively utilized in nursing homes, family care-givers might be less anxious about institutionalizing a family member for whom they can no longer provide care. This would be especially true if the PCA were already known to the resident through prior experience in the home care setting.

Specialized dementia care in all settings

Dementia care at home, or in an assisted living facility, is fraught with difficulties. Some of the support services available for disabled older adults, like adult day care, become problematic in the more advanced stages of the condition. It is difficult to get sustained psychotherapeutic help at home for mental health co-morbidities like depression and anxiety if there is little hope of rehabilitation. Drugs become the solution by default. Family members and PCAs can get frustrated by the many behavioral problems they face, as described in Chapter Three.

The burden can be reduced, however, with competent formal caregiving. Studies have shown that if healthcare professionals, family members, and formal caregivers are given adequate training in dementia, they can better understand the nature of the disease and its progression (Cherry, 2012). They can learn how to determine whether the elder has a real or only apparent comprehension of a given situation. They will better understand the source of behavioral problems and how to address them. They will also better understand the susceptibility of dementia patients to injuries, mental health conditions, and medical problems.

Properly trained PCAs can mitigate this problem, in homes and in assisted living residences, and should be considered a major component of any agenda for expanding personal care services.

SCUs in all nursing homes

The unique aspects of dementia care and the need for specialized training makes it imperative that all nursing homes develop specialized care units based on the Oregon model described in Chapter Five. Families faced with institutionalizing a loved one must feel confident that she is getting the best possible care and studies have already shown that SCUs and specialized training can significantly improve outcomes and satisfaction.

PCAs with dementia training can help in the SCU environment as well, given the high level of need for one-to-one care and limits on CNA availability.

More geriatric health professionals

Geriatric healthcare is complex. Physicians, nurses, and other professionals face patients with multiple chronic conditions using multiple medications. It is not unusual for an older adult to be under the care of a half dozen separate medical specialists at one time. It is also expected that the oldest old will develop new conditions, see other conditions worsen, and undergo a number of healthcare transitions, into rehabilitation, nursing care, palliative care, and hospice care.

One of the major advantages of the PACE program is its ability to bring together multiple providers into a single system with a dedicated physician leader working with an accessible online patient history and profile. Successful caring for older adults requires geriatric specialists to coordinate the complex and shifting world of aging.

Chapter Four noted the serious shortfalls in geriatric specialties as enumerated by the Institute of Medicine. With a fragmented and market-driven healthcare system, however, it will be difficult for the U.S. to meet the future need. For example, as of 2014 there were only 8 full geriatrics departments in the 145 academic medical centers in the U.S. (Baruchin, 2015). In the United Kingdom, by way of contrast, all medical schools are required to have a geriatrics department. U.S. medical schools are licensed by 50 separate states and accredited by private, non-profit agencies that provide only very general guidelines. It will be difficult to introduce systemic and deep curriculum change.

Non-profit organizations, like the Hartford Foundation and Robert Wood Johnson Foundation, raise grant money from government and other sources to develop needed geriatric training programs, but this is not nearly enough. Providing effective care coordination and management for aging boomers to make aging in place possible, will require a massive increase in the number of trained professionals and in relatively short order. This can be accomplished through added training and education, and through meaningful incentives intended to bring more professionals into geriatric practice:

Geriatrics education in medical and nursing schools: Over recent years, accrediting bodies for medical and nursing education have asked their institutions to increase the number of curriculum units in geriatric theory and clinical practice (e.g., American Association of Colleges of Nursing, 2015). They have left it to the institutions to determine how to best do this. With little room in an already tight core curriculum, however, many institutions are doing very little. Some are creating only electives, or are simply adding geriatric examples to existing courses (Bardach & Rowles, 2012). The federal government needs to establish a meaningful mandate for institutions that use federal grants or are approved to process federal financial aid for students. At least some geriatrics courses should be changed from electives to required courses and institutions should be required to have a full-time geriatrics educator on staff to work with departments to infuse the broader curriculum with essential geriatrics units, including clinical practice opportunities.

Geriatrics continuing education: The federal government should insist that all states require that current primary care physicians take a set number of continuing education units (CEUs) each year in geriatrics and gerontology and that new primary care physicians take enough CEUs to remedy deficiencies in their medical education. Nurses should have similar requirements. In addition, educators in medical and nursing schools should be required to take such courses along with continuing education courses that address faculty and curriculum development in this area.

Incentives for entering eldercare fields: As discussed in Chapter Four, current incentives used to coax medical and nursing students to enter geriatric practice are not working. Medicare reimbursement levels must continue to be adjusted upward to fix the problem and new incentives should be added. Some federal student loan debt is currently forgiven for primary care physicians who work in poor communities. This should be expanded to include geriatric practice across all communities.

The need for public awareness

Under ideal conditions, caring for an older relative can be a fulfilling experience. In less than ideal conditions, however, the situation changes significantly. A 2009 survey by the National Alliance for Caregiving and AARP found that 43% of all family caregivers were doing the work not because it was fulfilling but because they felt they had no choice, for any number of reasons. They indicated a strong interest in sharing the responsibility with others (National Alliance for Caregiving & AARP, 2009). A similar survey in 2030–2050 would likely see this percentage rise dramatically.

The 2030 crisis is forcing us, as a nation, to address this need for shared responsibility. The problem is bigger than any one person. Disability, dementia, and depression can afflict an older adult in any segment of society and inflict emotional distress in even the wealthiest.

If everyone recognizes the problem and wants a solution, obstacles associated with budgets and finance can be overcome. They were overcome when Social Security and Medicare were first developed. They were overcome in World War II. The crisis cannot be addressed without better pay and training for direct care workers and without providing round-the-clock care in a home setting. The crisis cannot be addressed without expanding nursing homes and special care units, and improving their staffing and conditions. The crisis cannot be addressed without providing financial support to family caregivers forced to leave the workforce to care for a loved one.

Caregivers suffer in silence. Advocates for the aging and their caregivers, still stinging from the demise of the CLASS program, struggle to win small gains in states paralyzed by budget shortfalls and political inertia. The current national political and economic landscape does not look good for implementing a major expansion of social services.

With increased public awareness, however, based on a true common interest, the caregiver problem can be elevated and garner a bipartisan consensus for urgent national action. Maintaining the health and emotional well-being of aging adults and their family caregivers is a public value of the highest order.

References

AARP. (2012). *Boomers and the Great Recession: Struggling to recover.* Washington, D.C.: AARP Public Policy Institute. Retrieved at: http://www.aarp.org/content/dam/aarp/research/public_policy_institute/econ_sec/2012/boomers-and-the-great-recession-struggling-to-recover-v2-AARP-ppi-econ-sec.pdf

AARP. (2014). *Caregiving among Asian Americans and Pacific Islanders Age 50+.* Washington, D.C.: AARP Research Center. Retrieved at: http://www.aarp.org/content/dam/aarp/home-and-family/caregiving/2014-11/report_caregiving_aapis_english.pdf

Abrahamson, K., Clark, D., Perkins, A. & Arling, G. (2012). Does cognitive impairment influence quality of life among nursing home residents? *The Gerontologist, 52*(5), 632-640.

Abrahamson, K., Lewis, T., Perkins, A., Clark, D., Nazir, A., & Arling, G. (2013). The influence of cognitive impairment, special care unit placement, and nursing facility characteristics on resident quality of life. *Journal of Aging and Health, 25*(4), 574-588.

Adler, N. & Newman, K. (2002). Socioeconomic disparities in health: pathways and policies. *Health Affairs, 21*(2), 60-76.

Alcorn, K. (2014, January 8). Millennials want children but they're not planning on them. *The New York Times.* Retrieved online

at the New York Times website: http://parenting.blogs.
nytimes.com/2014/01/08/millennials-want-children-but-they-
re-not-planning-on them/?_r=2&utm_source=World+-
Congress+of+Families+and+The+Howard+Center+for+-
Family%2C+Religion+%26+Society+Members&utm_cam-
paign=83e709b264-NFNR_Nordic_Country_Rethinks_
Divorce&utm_medium=email&utm_term=0_4b0ced8706-83e7
09b264-342040565

Alecxih, L. (2006). *Nursing home use by "oldest old" sharply declines*
(Report). Falls Church, VA: The Lewin Group. Retrieved at the
Lewin Group website: http://www.lewin.com/~/media/Lewin/Site_
Sections/Publications/NursingHomeUseTrendsPaperRev.pdf

Allen, N., Siddique, J., Wilkins, J., Shay, C., Lewis, C., Goff, D. ... Lloyd-
Jones, D. (2014). Blood pressure trajectories in early adulthood and
subclinical atherosclerosis in middle age. *Journal of the American
Medical Association, 311*(5), 490-497.

Allen, S., Foster, A., & Berg, K. (2001). Receiving help at home: The
interplay of human and technological assistance. *The Journals of
Gerontology Series B, 56B*(6), S374-S382.

Alzheimer's Association. (2012). 2012 Alzheimer's disease facts and
figures. *Alzheimer's and Dementia, 8*(2). Retrieved from the
Alzheimer's Association website: https://www.alz.org/documents_
custom/2012_facts_figures_fact_sheet.pdf

Alzheimer's Association. (2014a). *Staying safe* (Brochure). Retrieved from
the Alzheimer's Association website: https://www.alz.org/national/
documents/brochure_stayingsafe.pdf

Alzheimer's Association. (2014b). 2014 Alzheimer's disease facts and
figures. *Alzheimer's and Dementia, 10*(2). Retrieved from the
Alzheimer's Association website: http://www.alz.org/downloads/
facts_figures_2014.pdf

Alzheimer's Association. (2015). 2015 Alzheimer's disease facts and figures. *Alzheimer's and Dementia, 11*(3). Retrieved for the Alzheimer's Association website: https://www.alz.org/facts/downloads/facts_figures_2015.pdf

American Association of Colleges of Nursing. (2015). *Competencies to improve care for older adults.* Washington, D.C.: American Association of Colleges of Nursing (AACN). Retrieved from the AACN website: http://www.aacn.nche.edu/education-resources/competencies-older-adults

American Elder Care Research Organization. (2015, April). *Paying for aging care by converting a life insurance policy.* Reno, NV: American Elder Care Research Organization (AECR). Retrieved from the AECR Paying for Senior Care website: http://www.payingforseniorcare.com/longtermcare/lifecare-assurance-benefit-plan.html

American Federation for Aging Research. (n.d.). *Centers for Excellence.* New York, NY: American Federation for Aging Research (AFAR). Retrieved from the AFAR website at http://www.afar.org/research/centers/

American Health Care Association. (2014). *American Health Care Association 2012 Staffing Report.* Washington, D.C.: American Health Care Association (AHCA). Retrieved from the AHCA website: http://www.ahcancal.org/research_data/staffing/Documents/2012_Staffing_Report.pdf

Ancoli-Israel, S. & Roth. T. (1999). Characteristics of insomnia in the United States: Results of the 1991 National Sleep Foundation Survey. *Sleep, 22*(S2), S347-353.

Anesbensel, C., Pearlin, L., Mullan, J., Zarit, S., & Whitlatch, C. (1995). *Profiles in caregiving: The unexpected career.* San Diego, CA: Academic Press.

Arellano, J. (2015). Don't leave the United States behind: Problems with the existing Family and Medical Leave Act, and alternatives to enhance the employee work-family relationship in the 21ˢᵗ Century. *Journal of Workplace Rights.* Retrieved from the Sage Publications website: http://sgo.sagepub.com/content/spsgo/5/2/2158244015581553.full.pdf

Barbarotta, L. (2010). *Direct care worker retention: Strategies for success.* Washington, D.C.: Leading Age (formerly the American Association of Homes and Services for the Aging), Institute for the Future of Aging Services. Retrieved from the Leading Age website: http://www.leadingage.org/uploadedFiles/Content/About/Center_for_Applied_Research/Publications_and_Products/Direct%20Care%20Workers%20Report%20%20FINAL%20(2).pdf

Bardach, S. & Rowles, G. (2012). Geriatrics education in the health professions: Are we making progress? *The Gerontologist, 52*(5), 607-618.

Baruchin, A. (2015, April). *More seniors, fewer geriatricians: Shifting demographics pose challenges for medical education.* Washington, D.C.: American Association of Medical Colleges (AAMC). Retrieved at the AAMC website: https://www.aamc.org/newsroom/reporter/april2015/429722/fewer-geriatricians.html

Bates-Jensen, B., Schnelle, J., Alessi, C., Al-Samarrai, N., & Levy-Storms, L. (2004). The effects of staffing on in-bed times of nursing home residents. *Journal of the American Geriatrics Society, 52*(6), 931-938.

Beauchamp, J., Cheh, V., Schmitz, R., Kemper, P., & Hall, J. (2008). *The effect of the Program of All-inclusive Care for the Elderly (PACE) on quality.* (Report prepared under contract #500-00-0033 (01) between the Centers for Medicare and Medicaid Services [CMS] and Mathematica Policy Research, Inc.). Washington, D.C.: U.S. Department of Health and Human Services, Centers for Medicare

and Medicaid Services. Retrieved from the CMS website: https://
www.cms.gov/Research-Statistics-Data-and-Systems/Statistics-
Trends-and-Reports/Reports/downloads/beauchamp_2008.pdf

Bell, K. (2015). *Tax help in caring for aging parents*. New York, NY:
Bankrate Inc. Retrieved from the Bankrate website: http://www.
bankrate.com/finance/taxes/tax-help-in-caring-for-an-aging-par-
ent-1.aspx

Birrer, R., & Vemuri, S. (2004). Depression in later life: A diagnostic
and therapeutic challenge. *American Family Physician, 69*(10),
2375-2382.

Bishop, C., & Stone, R. (2014). Implications for policy: The nursing home
as least restrictive setting. *The Gerontologist, 54*(S1), S98-S103.

Blaum, C., Xue, Q., Michelon, E., Semba, R., & Fried, L. (2005). The asso-
ciation between obesity and the frailty syndrome in older women:
The women's health and aging studies. *Journal of the American
Geriatrics Society, 53*(6), 927-934.

Blazer, D. (2003). Depression in late life: Review and commentary. *Journal
of Gerontology, 58A*(23), 249-265.

Bobby, C. & Urofsky, R. (2008, August). CACREP adopts new standards. *Counseling Today* (online). Alexandria, VA: Council on
Accreditation for Counseling and Related Education Programs
(CACREP). Retrieved from the CACREP website: http://www.
cacrep.org/wp-content/uploads/2012/07/CACREP-adopts-new-
standards-August-2008.pdf

Brown, S. & Lin, I-F. (2012). The gray divorce revolution: Rising divorce
among middle-aged and older adults, 1990-2010. *The Journals of
Gerontology Series B, 67*(6), 731-741.

Buhr, G. & Paniagua, M. (2011). Update on teaching in the long-term
care setting. *Clinical Geriatric Medicine, 27*(2), 199-211.

Cadigan, R., Grabowski, D., Givens, J., & Mitchell, S. (2012). The quality of advanced dementia care in the nursing home: The role of special care units. *Medical Care, 50*(10), 856-862.

Caffrey C, Sengupta M., Park-Lee, E., Moss, A., Rosenoff, E., & Harris-Kojetin, L. (2012*). Residents living in residential care facilities: United States, 2010* (Data brief, no. 91). Hyattsville, MD: U.S. Department of Health and Human Services, Centers for Disease Control and Prevention (CDC). Retrieved from the CDC website: http://www.cdc.gov/nchs/data/databriefs/db91.pdf

Cambois, E., Blachier, A., & Robine, J-M. (2012). Aging and health in France: An unexpected expansion of disability in mid-adulthood over recent years. *European Journal of Public Health, 136,* 575-581.

Carlson, B., Foster, L., Dale, S., & Brown, R. (2007). Effects of cash and counseling on personal care and well-being. *Health Services Research, 42*(1 Pt. 2), 467-487.

Cassidy, K-L., & Rector, N. (2008). The silent geriatric giant: Anxiety disorders in late life. *Geriatrics and Aging, 11*(3), 150-156.

Castle, N. (2008). Special care units and their influence on nursing home occupancy characteristics. *Health Care Management Review, 33(1),* 79-91.

Castle, N. (2011, September). The cost of turnover (Conference presentation). *Advancing Excellence in America's Nursing Homes.* Washington, D.C.: Advancing Excellence in Long-Term Care. Retrieved from the Kentucky Association of Health Care Facilities website: https://www.kahcf.org/files/Nick%20Castle%20Slides%20on%20Staff%20Turnover%20and%20AE%20Campaign%200911.ppt

CDC. (2010). *Number of Americans with Diabetes projected to double or triple by 2050* (Press release). Washington, D.C.: U.S. Department of Health and Human Services, Centers for Disease Control and

Prevention (CDC). Retrieved at the CDC website: http://www.cdc.
gov/media/pressrel/2010/r101022.html

CDC. (2013). *Trends in current cigarette smoking among high school
students and adults, United States, 1965-2011* (Statistical report).
Washington, D.C.: U.S. Department of Health and Human Services,
Centers for Disease Control and Prevention (CDC). Retrieved
at the CDC website: http://www.cdc.gov/tobacco/data_statistics/
tables/trends/cig_smoking/

CDC. (2014). *Arthritis-related statistics* (Statistical report). Washington,
D.C.: U.S. Department of Health and Human Services, Centers for
Disease Control and Prevention (CDC). Retrieved at the CDC website: http://www.cdc.gov/arthritis/data_statistics/arthritis_related_
stats.htm

CDC. (2015a). Older adult falls: Get the facts (Statistical report).
Washington, D.C.: U.S. Department of Health and Human Services,
Centers for Disease Control and Prevention (CDC). Retrieved at
the CDC website: http://www.cdc.gov/homeandrecreationalsafety/
falls/adultfalls.html

CDC. (2015b). *Costs of falls among older adults* (Statistical report).
Washington, D.C.: U.S. Department of Health and Human Services,
Centers for Disease Control and Prevention (CDC). Retrieved at
the CDC website: http://www.cdc.gov/HomeandRecreationalSafety/
Falls/fallcost.html

Center for Medicare Education. (2001). *The PACE model* (Issue
Brief), 2(10). Washington, D.C.: U.S. Department of Health
and Human Services, Centers for Medicare and Medicaid
Services. Retrieved from the National PACE association website: http://old.npaonline.org/website/download.
asp?id=743&title=%22The_PACE_Model%22

Center for Excellence in Assisted Living. (2015). *The future of assisted living in the era of healthcare reform* (Summary of an October, 2014 Washington, D.C. symposium). Oakton, VA: Center for Excellence in Assisted Living (CEAL). Retrieved from the CEAL website: http://www.theceal.org/images/white-papers/CEAL-White-Paper-Formatted-FINAL-033115v3.pdf

Centers for Medicare and Medicaid Services. (2014). *Nursing home quality initiative: Quality measures*. Washington, D.C.: U.S. Department of Health and Human Services, Centers for Medicare and Medicaid Services (CMS). Retrieved from the CMS website: https://www.cms.gov/Medicare/Quality-Initiatives-Patient-Assessment-instruments/NursingHomeQualityInits/NHQIQualityMeasures.html

Centers for Medicare and Medicaid Services. (2015, February 20) *CMS strengthens five-star rating system for nursing homes* (Press release). Washington, D.C.: U.S. Department of Health and Human Services, Centers for Medicare and Medicaid Services (CMS). Retrieved from the CMS website: https://www.cms.gov/Newsroom/MediaReleaseDatabase/Press-releases/2015-Press-releases-items/2015-02-20-2.html

Chatterji, P., Burstein, N., Kidder, D., White, A. (1998). The impact of PACE on participant Outcomes (Report based on contract no. 500-96-0003/TO4 between the National Health Care Financing Administration and Abt Associates): Washington, D.C.: U.S. Department of Health and Human Services, National Healthcare Financing Administration (now Centers for Disease Control and Prevention). Retrieved at the NPAonline website: https://www.cms.gov/Medicare/Demonstration-Projects/DemoProjectsEvalRpts/downloads/PACE_Outcomes.pdf

Cherry, D. (2012). HCBS can keep people with dementia at home. *Generations, 36*(1), 83-90.

Clegg, A., Young, J., Iliffe, S., Rikkert, M., & Rockwood, K. (2013). Frailty in elderly people. *The Lancet, 381*, 752-762.

Colello, K. & Mulvey, J. (2013). *Community Living Assistance Services and Supports (CLASS): Overview and summary of provisions* (Report to Congress). Washington, D.C.: U.S. Congress, Congressional Research Service. Retrieved from the National Conference of State Legislatures website: http://www.ncsl.org/documents/statefed/ health/CLASSOvrview21313.pdf

Congressional Budget Office. (2013). *Rising demand for long-term services and supports* (Report prepared for the U.S. Senate Committee on Finance). Washington, D.C.: U.S. Congress, Congressional Budget Office (CBO). Retrieved from the CBO website: https://www.cbo. gov/sites/default/files/113th-congress-2013-2014/reports/44363- LTC.pdf

Connolly, C. (2015). *Aging in place will require investing in home care workers* (Fact Sheet). New York, NY: National Employment Law Center (NELP). Retrieved from the NELP website: http://www.nelp.org/publication/ aging-in-place-will-require-investing-in-home-care-workers/

Crane, P., Walker, R., Hubbard, R., Li, G., Nathan, D., Zheng, H. ... Larson, E. (2013). Glucose levels and risk of dementia. *New England Journal of Medicine, 369*, 540-548.

Crowson, C., Matteson, E., Davis, J., & and Gabriel, S. (2013). Contribution of obesity to the rise in incidence of rheumatoid arthritis. *Arthritis Care Research, 65*(1), 71-77.

Council on Social Work Education. (2009). *Why recruit students to gerontological social Work* (Fact Sheet). Alexandria, VA.: Council on

Social Work Education (CSWE). Retrieved from the CSWE web-site: http://www.cswe.org/File.aspx?id=31797

Day, T. (2010). *About nursing homes*. West Bountiful, UT: National Care Planning Council (NCPC). Retrieved from the NCPC website: https://www.longtermcarelink.net/eldercare/nursing_home.htm

Dean, A., Kolody, B., Wood, P., & Matt, G. (1992). The influence of living alone on depression in elderly persons. *Journal of Aging Health*, 4(1), 3-18.

Derman, P., Fabricant, P., & David, G. (2014). The role of overweight and obesity in relation to the more rapid growth of total knee arthro-plasty volume compared with total hip arthroplasty volume. *Journal of Bone and Joint Surgery*, 96(11), 922-928.

Doraiswamy, P., Leon, J., Cummings, L., Marin, D., & Neumann, P. (2002). Prevalence and impact of medical comorbidity in Alzheimer's disease. *The Journals of Gerontology Series A*, 57(3), M173-M177.

Doty, M., Koren, M., & Sturla, E. (2008). *Culture change in nursing homes: How far have we come? Findings from the Commonwealth Fund 2007 National Survey of Nursing Homes (Report no. 1131)*. Washington, D.C.: The Commonwealth Fund (CF). Retrieved from the CF website: http://www.commonwealthfund.org/usr_doc/ Doty_culturechangenursinghomes_1131.pdf?section=4039

Eden, J., Maslow, K., Le, M., Blazer, D., eds. (2012). *The Mental Health and Substance Use Workforce for Older Adults: In whose hands?* Washington, D.C.: Institute of Medicine, National Academies Press.

Egge, R. (2013). *Open letter to the Long-Term Care Commission*. Chicago, IL: Alzheimer's Association. Retrieved at the Alzheimer's Association website: http://www.alz.org/national/documents/Long-Term-Care-Commission-8-16-13.pdf

Eiken, S., Sredl, K., Burwell, B., & Saucier, P. (2015). *Medicaid expenditures for long-term services and supports (LTSS) in FY 2013: Home and community-based services were a majority of LTSS spending* (Report under contract HHSM-500-2010-000261 between the U.S. Department of Health and Human Services and Mathematica Policy Research). Washington, D.C.: U.S. Department of Health and Human Services, Centers for Medicare and Medicaid Services. Retrieved from the Medicaid website: http://www.medicaid.gov/medicaid-chip-program-information/by-topics/long-term-services-and-supports/downloads/ltss-expenditures-fy2013.pdf

Eldercare Workforce Alliance. (2014). *Advanced Direct Care Worker: A role to improve quality and efficiency of care for older adults and strengthen career ladders for home care workers* (Issue brief). Washington, D.C.: Eldercare Workforce Alliance (EWA). Retrieved at the EWA website: http://www.eldercareworkforce.org/research/issue-briefs/research:advanced-dcw-brief/

Eliopoulos, C. (2013a). Let's open our eyes to the barriers to culture change. *Annals of Long-Term Care, 21*(12), 44-45.

Eliopoulos, C. (2013b). Affecting culture change and performance improvement in Medicaid nursing homes: The Promote Understanding, Leadership, and Learning (PULL) program. *Geriatric Nursing, 34*(3), 218-223.

Eljay LLC & Hansen Hunter and Company. (2015). *A report on shortfalls in Medicaid funding for nursing center care* (Research report). Washington, D.C.: American Health Care Association (AHCA). Retrieved from the AHCA website: http://www.ahcancal.org/research_data/funding/Documents/2014%20Medicaid%20Underfunding%20for%20Nursing%20Center%20Care%20FINAL.pdf

Engel, S., Kiely, D., & Mitchell, S. (2008). Satisfaction with end-of-life care for nursing home residents with advanced dementia. *Journal of the American Geriatrics Society, 54*(10), 1567-1572.

Engquist, G., Johnson, C., Lind, A., & Barnette, L. (2010). *Medicaid-funded long-term care: Toward more home and community-based options* (Policy brief). Hamilton, NJ: Center for Health Care Strategies (CHCS). Retrieved from the CHCS website: http://www.chcs.org/media/LTSS_Policy_Brief_.pdf

Fernandez, F. (2006). Sundowning and delirium (Conference presentation). *Geriatric Psychiatry for the Primary Care Physician*, organized by the Carter-Jenkins Center and the University of South Florida, Tampa, FL, March, 2006. Retrieved from the Carter-Jenkins Center website: www.thecjc.org/ppoint/ppoint/gc06-3.ppt

Fishman, M., Barnow, B., Glosser, A., & Gardiner, K. (2004). *Recruiting and retaining a quality paraprofessional long-term care workforce: Building collaboratives with the nation's Workforce Investment System* (Report prepared under contract #100-03-0009 between the Office of Disability, Aging and Long-Term Care Policy [DALTCP] and the Future of Aging Services). Washington, D.C.: U.S. Department of Health and Human Services (HHS), DALTCP. Retrieved from the HHS Assistant Secretary of Planning and Evaluation website: http://aspe.hhs.gov/daltcp/reports/natwis.htm

Folbre, N. & Wolf, D. (2012). Long-term care coverage for all: Getting there from here. In D. Wolf and N. Folbre (eds.), *Universal coverage of long-term care in the United States: Can we get there from here?* (e-book). New York, NY: Russell Sage Foundation (RSF), pp. 217-239. Retrieved from the RSF website: https://www.russellsage.org/sites/all/files/WolfFolbreuniversal.pdf

Freedman, V., Spillman, B., Andreski, P., Comman, J., Crimmins, E., Kramarow, E. ...Waidman, T. (2013). Trends in late-life activity limitations in the United States: An update from five national surveys. *Demography, 50*(2), 661-671.

Freedman, V. & Spillman, B. (2014). Disability and care needs among older Americans. *Milbank Quarterly, 92*(3), 509-541.

Fried, L., Tangen, C., Walston, J., Newman, A., Hirsch, C., Gottdiener, J. ... McBurnie, M. (2001). Frailty in older adults: Evidence for a phenotype. *The Journals of Gerontology Series A, 56A*(3), M146-156.

Gallagher, L. (2011). *The high cost of poor care: The financial case for prevention in American nursing homes* (Report). Washington, D.C.: National Consumer Voice for Quality Long-term Care. Retrieved from the Consumer Voice website: http://theconsumervoice.org/uploads/files/issues/The-High-Cost-of-Poor-Care.pdf

General Accounting Office. (2003). *Long-term care: Federal Oversight of growing Medicaid home and community-based waivers should be strengthened* (Report to Congressional Requesters). Washington, D.C.: U.S. Government, General Accounting Office (GAO). Retrieved at the GAO website: http://www.gao.gov/new.items/d03576.pdf

Getz, L. (2010). Eliminating bedsores. *Aging Well, 3*(3), p. 20. Retrieved from Today's Geriatric Medicine website: http://www.todaysgeriatricmedicine.com/archive/082510p20.shtml

Ghosh, A., Schmitz, R., & Brown, R. (2015). *Effect of PACE on costs, nursing home admissions, and mortality: 2006-2011* (Report prepared under contract #HHSP23320095642WC between the Office of Disability, Aging and Long-Term Care Policy [DALTCP] and Mathematica Policy Research). Washington, D.C.: U.S. Department of Health and Human Services (HHS), Office of Disability, Aging and Long-Term Care Policy. Retrieved from the HHS Assistant Secretary for Planning and Evaluation website: http://aspe.hhs.gov/basic-report/

effect-pace-costs-nursing-home-admissions-and-mortal-
ity-2006-2011

Golant, S. (2008). The future of assisted living residences: A response to uncertainty. In S. Golant & J. Hyde (eds.), *The assisted living residence: A vision for the future* (pp. 3-45). Baltimore, MD: The Johns Hopkins University Press.

Golden, J., Conroy, R., Bruce, I., Denihan, A., Greene, E., Kirby, M., & Lawlor, B. (2011). The spectrum of worry in the community dwelling elderly. *Aging and Mental Health, 15*(8), 985-994.

Gomaa, A., Tapp, L, Luckhaupt, S., Vanoli, K., Sarmiento, R., Raudabaugh, W. ... Sprigg, S. (2015). Occupational traumatic injuries among workers in healthcare facilities – United States 2012-2014. *CDC Mortality and Morbidity Weekly Report, 64*(15), 405-410.

Grabowski, D., Elliot, A., Leitzell, B., Cohen, L., & Zimmerman, S. (2014a). Who are the innovators? Nursing homes implementing culture change. *The Gerontologist, 54*(supplement 1), S65-S75.

Grabowski, D., O'Malley, J., Afendulis, C., Caudry, D., Elliot, A., & Zimmerman, S. (2014b). Culture change and nursing home quality of care. *The Gerontologist, 54*(supplement 1), S35-S45.

Graham, J. (2013, October 14). California imposes new home care regulations (Blog post). *New York Times*. Retrieved from New York Times website: http://newoldage.blogs.nytimes.com/2013/10/14/california-imposes-new-home-care-regulations/

Grande, M. (2003). Special care units: History, regulation, and criticism. *Marquette Elder's Adviser, 4*(3), Article 6.

Grant, L. (2008). *Culture change in a for-profit nursing home chain: An evaluation* (Research report). Washington, D.C.: The Commonwealth Fund (CF). Retrieved from the CF website: http://

www.commonwealthfund.org/publications/fund-reports/2008/feb/culture-change-in-a-for-profit-nursing-home-chain--an-evaluation

Green House Project. (2011, September 8). *RWJF announces $10 million program related investment (PRI) to expand Green House access to low-income elders* (Blog post). Arlington, VA: The Green House Project. Retrieved from the Green House Project website: http://blog.thegreenhouseproject.org/rwjf-announce-10-million-expand-green-house-access-to-low-income-elders/

Green House Project. (2015). *Vision/mission.* Retrieved from the Green House Project website: http://www.thegreenhouseproject.org/about/visionmission

Gregory, S. (2001). *The nursing home workforce: Certified nurse assistants* (Report). Washington, D.C.: AARP Public Policy Institute. Retrieved from the AARP website: http://www.aarp.org/home-garden/livable-communities/info-2001/aresearch-import-688-FS86.html

Gorelick, P., Scuteri, A., Black, S., DeCarli, C., Greenberg, S., Iadecola, C. ... Seshadri, S. (2011). Vascular contributions to cognitive impairment and dementia: A statement for health professionals from the American Heart Association and the American Stroke Association. *Stroke, 42,* 2672-2713.

Gruneir, A., Lapane, K., Miller, S., & Mor V. (2007). Long-term care market competition and nursing home dementia special care units. *Medical Care, 45*(8), 739-745.

Gruneir, A., Lapane, K., Miller, S., & Mor, V. (2008). Is dementia care really special? A new look at an old question. *Journal of the American Geriatrics Society, 56*(2), 199-205.

Guo, J. (2014). *Is expanding public-financed home care cost-effective?* (Issue brief). Washington, D.C.: American Institutes for Research (AIR), Center on Aging. Retrieved from the AIR website: http://www.air.

org/sites/default/files/downloads/report/Expanding%20Public%20
Financed%20Home%20Care_Oct%202014.pdf

Hall, C., Derby, C, LeValley, A., Katz, M., Verghese, J., & Lipton, R.
(2007). Education delays accelerated decline on a memory test in
persons who develop dementia. *Neurology, 69*(17), 1657-64.

Harrington, C. (2002). *Nursing home staffing standards* (Issue paper).
Menlo Park, CA: Kaiser Family Foundation (KFF), Kaiser
Commission on Medicaid and the Uninsured. Retrieved from
the KFF website: https://kaiserfamilyfoundation.files.wordpress.
com/2002/08/nursing-home-staffing-standards.pdf

Harvard School of Public Health–MetLife Foundation. (2004).
Reinventing aging: Baby boomers and civic engagement (Report).
Cambridge, MA: Harvard School of Public Health, Center for
Health Communication. Retrieved from the AARP website: http://
assets.aarp.org/rgcenter/general/boomers_engagement.pdf

Hebert, L., Weuve, J., Scherr, P. & Evans, D. (2013). Alzheimer disease in
the United States (2010–2050) estimated using the 2010 census.
Neurology, 80, 1778-83.

Hernandez-Medina, E., Eaton, S., Hurd, D., & White, A. (2006). *Training
programs for nursing assistants* (Report no. 2006-08). Washington
D.C.: AARP Public Policy Institute. Retrieved from the AARP website: http://assets.aarp.org/rgcenter/il/2006_08_cna.pdf

Hess, C. & Henrici, J. (2013). *Increasing pathways to legal status for immigrant in-home care workers* (Research report). Washington, D.C.:
Institute for Women's Policy Research (IWPR). Retrieved from the
IWPR website: http://www.iwpr.org/carousel/increasing-pathways-
to-legal-status-for-immigrant-in-home-care-workers

Holmes, D. (2015). Nursing homes: Special care units. *Jrank Medicine
Encyclopedia Online.* Retrieved from the Jrank website: http://

medicine.jrank.org/pages/1244/Nursing-Homes-Special-Care-Units.html

Home Care Pulse. (2015). *Highlights of the Private Duty Benchmarking Study*. Rexburg, ID: Home Care Pulse Benchmarking Studies. Retrieved from the Home Care Pulse website: http://benchmarking.homecarepulse.com/

Hubbard, R., Lang, I., Llewellyn, D., & Rockwood, K. (2010). Frailty, body mass index, and abdominal obesity in older people. *The Journals of Gerontology Series A, 65*(4), 377-381.

Huelsman, M. (2015). *The debt divide: Racial and class bias behind the "new normal" of student Borrowing* (Research report). New York, NY: Demos. Retrieved from the Demos website: http://www.demos.org/publication/debt-divide-racial-and-class-bias-behind-new-normal-student-borrowing

Hwang, T., Masterman, D., Ortiz, F., Fairbanks, L., & Cummings, J. (2004). Mild cognitive impairment is associated with characteristic neuropsychiatric symptoms. *Alzheimer Disease and Associated Disorders, 18*(1), 17-21.

Hybels, C., Pieper, C., & Blazer, D. (2009). The complex relationship between depressive symptoms and functional limitations in community-dwelling older adults: The impact of subthreshold depression. *Psychological Medicine, 39*, 1677-1688.

Iadecola, C. & Davisson, R. (2008). Hypertension and cerebrovascular dysfunction. *Cell Metabolism, 7*(6), 476-484.

Institute of Medicine. 2008. *Retooling for an Aging America*. Washington, D.C.: Institute of Medicine, National Academies Press.

Kaiser Family Foundation. (2012). *Medicaid benefits: Personal care services* (Medicaid Benefits Data Report). Menlo Park, CA: Kaiser

Family Foundation (KFF). Retrieved from the KFF website: http://
kff.org/medicaid/state-indicator/personal-care-services/

Kaiser Family Foundation. (2013). *Overview of nursing facility capacity,*
financing, and ownership in the United States in 2011 (Report).
Menlo Park, CA: Kaiser Family Foundation (KFF). Retrieved
from the KFF website: http://kff.org/medicaid/fact-sheet/
overview-of-nursing-facility-capacity-financing-and-owner-
ship-in-the-united-states-in-2011/

Kane, R., Homyak, P., Bershadsky, B., & Flood, S. (2006). The effects
of a variant of the Program for All-inclusive Care for the Elderly
on hospital utilization and outcomes. *Journal of the American*
Geriatrics Society, 54(2), 276-283.

Kapes, B. (2013). *Depression and baby boomers: How having it all may be*
too much. Newburyport, MA: PsychCentral. Retrieved from the
PsychCentral.org website: http://psychcentral.com/lib/depression-
and-baby-boomers-how-having-it-all-may-be-too-much/

Kapp, M. (2014). Home and community-based long-term services
and supports: Health reform's most enduring legacy? *Saint Louis*
University Journal of Health Law and Policy, 8(1), 9-34.

Kaye, S., LaPlante, M., & Harrington, C. (2009). Do noninstitutional
long-term care services reduce Medicaid spending? *Health Affairs,*
28(1), 262-272.

Kelly, C., Morgan, J., & Jason, K. (2013). Home care workers: Interstate
differences in training requirements and their implications for
quality. *Journal of Applied Gerontology, 32*(7), 804-832.

Khatutsky, G., Wiener, J., Anderson, W., Akhmerova, V., Jessup, E., &
Squillace, M. (2011). *Understanding direct care workers: A snap-*
shot of two of America's most important jobs, certified nursing
assistants and home health aides (Report prepared under contract
#HHSP23320095651WC between the Office of Disability, Aging

and Long-Term Care Policy [DALTCP] and RTI International). Washington, D.C.: U.S. Department of Health and Human Services, DALTCP. Retrieved from the Office of the Assistant Secretary for Planning website: http://aspe.hhs.gov/daltcp/reports/2011/cnachart.htm

Khatutsky, G., Wiener, J., Anderson, W., & Porell, F. (2012). *Work-related injuries among certified nursing assistants working in U.S. nursing homes* (RTI Press publication No. RR-0017-1204). Research Triangle Park, NC: RTI Press. Retrieved from the RTI website: www.rti.org/rtipress.

King, D., Matheson, E., Chirina, S., Shankar, A., & Broman-Fulks, J. (2013). The status of baby boomers' health in the United States: The healthiest generation? *JAMA Internal Medicine, 173*(5), 385-386.

Klinenberg, E., Torres, S., & Portacolone, E. (2013). *Aging alone in America* (Briefing paper). Austin, TX: Council on Contemporary Families (CCF). Retrieved from the CCF website: https://www.contemporaryfamilies.org/wp-content/uploads/2013/10/2012_Briefing_Klinenberg_Aging-alone-in-america.pdf

Knickman, J. & Snell, E. (2002). The 2030 problem: Caring for aging baby boomers. *Health Services Research, 37*(4), 840-884.

Kolus, K. (2012, March 27). LTC industry generates $259 billion in revenue during 2011. *Long-Term Living Magazine* (on line). Retrieved at the Long-Term Living Magazine website: http://www.ltlmagazine.com/news-item/ltc-industry-generates-259-billion-revenue-during-2011

Koton, S., Schneider, A., Rosamund, W., Shahar, E., Sang, Y., Gottesman, R., & Coresh, J. (2014). Stroke incidence and mortality trends in U.S. communities, 1987 to 2011. *Journal of the American Medical Association, 312*(3), 259-268.

Langston, C. (2012, December 20). *Decline in geriatric fellows defies pay boost: +10% = -10%* (Blog post). New York, NY: John A. Hartford Foundation, HealthAGEnda Blog. Retrieved at the John A. Hartford Foundation website: http://www.jhartfound.org/blog/decline-in-geriatric-fellows-defies-pay-boost-10-10/

Larson, E. & Langa, K. (2013). New insights into the dementia epidemic. *New England Journal of Medicine, 369,* 2275-2277

Leung, F., & Schnelle, J. (2008). Urinary and fecal incontinence in nursing home residence. *Gastroenterology Clinics of North America, 37*(3), 697-707.

Leveille, S., Wee, C., & Iezzoni, L. (2005). Trends in obesity and arthritis among baby boomers and their predecessors, 1971-2002. *American Journal of Public Health, 95*(9), 1607-1613.

Levinson, D. (2012). *Oversight of quality of care in Medicaid home and community-based services waiver programs.* (Special report OEI-02-08-00179). Washington, D.C.: U.S. Department of Health and Human Services, Office of Inspector General. Retrieved at the Office of Inspector General website: http://oig.hhs.gov/oei/reports/oei-02-08-00170.pdf

Linton, S. (2000). A review of psychological risk factors in back and neck pain. *Spine, 25*(9), 1148-56.

Llorente, M. (2013). *Management of behavioral disturbances in dementia* (Slide presentation). Miami, FL: University of Miami, Center for Aging. Retrieved from the website of the Center for Aging at the University of Miami: http://www.centeronaging.med.miami.edu/documents/Managing.pdf

Long-Term Care Commission. (2013). *A comprehensive approach to long-term services and supports.* (Alternative recommendations by several commissioners for the *2013 Commission on Long-term Care Report to Congress*). Willamantic, CT: Center for Medicare

Advocacy. Retrieved at the Center for Medicare Advocacy website: http://www.medicareadvocacy.org/wp-content/uploads/2013/10/ LTCCAlternativeReport.pdf

Long-Term Care Community Coalition. (2013). *Nursing home policy brief: Mandatory minimum state staffing requirements needed to protect nursing home residents now and in the future.* New York, NY: Long-Term Care Community Coalition (LTCCC). Retrieved from the LTCCC website: http://www.ltccc.org/publications/documents/ LTCCCNursingHomeStaffingPolicyBrief2013final_000.pdf

Long-Term Care Financing Collaborative. (2015). *Principles for Improving financing and delivery of long-term services and supports.* Washington, D.C.: Convergence Center for Policy Resolution. Retrieved from the Convergence website: http://www.convergen-cepolicy.org/wp-content/uploads/2015/07/LTCFC-Foundational-Principles-Final-070215.pdf

Lowenstein, J. (2014, November 12*). Analysis shows widespread discrepancies in staffing levels reported by nursing homes.* Washington, D.C.: Center for Public Integrity. Retrieved at the Center for Public Integrity website: http://www.publicintegrity. org/2014/11/12/16246/analysis-shows-widespread-discrepan-cies-staffing-levels-reported-nursing-homes

Lowenstein, J. (2015, February 23). *Feds announce changes in nurs-ing home rating system.* Washington, D.C.: Center for Public Integrity. Retrieved at the Center for Public Integrity web-site: http://www.publicintegrity.org/2015/02/23/16802/ feds-announce-changes-nursing-home-rating-system

Luo, H., Fang, X., Liao, Y., Elliot, A., & Zhang, X. (2010). Associations of special care units and outcomes of residents with dementia: 2004 national nursing home survey. *The Gerontologist, 50*(4), 509-518.

Lusardi, A. & Mitchell, O. (2006). *Baby boomer retirement security: The roles of planning, financial literacy, and housing wealth* (Working Paper no. 12585). Cambridge, MA: National Bureau of Economic Research (NBER). Retrieved from the NBER website: http://www.nber.org/papers/w12585.

Lynch, M., Hernandez, M., & Estes, C. (2008). PACE: Has it changed the chronic care paradigm? *Social Work in Public Health, 23*(4), 3-24.

Magaziner, J., Hawkes, W., Hebel, J., Zimmerman, S., Fox, K., Dolan, M. ... Kenzora, J. (2000). Recovery from hip fracture in eight areas of function. *The Journals of Gerontology Series A, 55*(9), M498-507.

Marquand, A. & Chapman, S. (2014). *The national landscape of personal care aide training standards* (Report). San Francisco, CA: University of California at San Francisco, Health Workforce Research Center. Retrieved from the Health Workforce Research Center website: http://healthworkforce.ucsf.edu/sites/healthworkforce.ucsf.edu/files/Report-The_National_Landscape_of_Personal_Care_Aide_Training_Standards.pdf

Marquardt, G., Bueter, K., & Motzek, T. (2014). Impact of the design of the built environment on people with dementia: An evidence-based review. *Health Environments Research and Design Journal, 8*(1), 127-157.

Martin, L., Freedman, V., Schoeni, R., & Andreski, P. (2010). Recent trends in disability and related chronic conditions among people ages fifty to sixty-four. *Health Affairs (Millwood), 29*(4), 725-731.

McCall, W. (2004). Sleep in the elderly: Burden, diagnosis, and treatment. *Primary Care Companion-Journal of Clinical Psychiatry, 6*, 9-20.

McCallion, P., Toseland, R., Lacey, D., & Banks, S. (1999). Educating nursing assistants to communicate more effectively with nursing home residents with dementia. *The Gerontologist, 39*(5), 546-558.

McCarthy, J. (2015). *Reports of depression treatment highest among baby boomers*. Washington, D.C.: Gallup. Retrieved from the Gallup organization website: http://www.gallup.com/poll/181364/reports-depression-treatment-highest-among-baby-boomers.aspx

McCaughey, D., McGhan, G., Kim, J., Brannon, D., Leroy, H., & Jablonski, R. (2012). Workforce implications of injury among home health workers: Evidence from the National Home Health Aide Survey. *The Gerontologist, 52*(4), 493-505.

McGuckin, N. & Lynott, J. (2010). *Impact of baby boomers on U.S. travel, 1969-2009* (Insight on the Issues Report 70). Washington, D.C.: AARP Public Policy Institute. Retrieved from the AARP website: http://www.aarp.org/content/dam/aarp/research/public_policy_institute/liv_com/2012/impact-baby-boomers-travel-1969-2009-AARP-ppi-liv-com.pdf

McKnight's Long-Term Care News. (2012, September 11). *Nursing home group heightens lobbying for Medicaid funding before November elections*. Retrieved from the McKnight's website: http://www.mcknights.com/news/nursing-home-group-heightens-lobbying-for-medicaid-funding-before-november-elections/article/258391/

Messier, S., Mihalko, S., Legault, C., Miller, G., Nicklas, B., DeVita, P. Beavers, D. ... Loeser, R. (2013). Effects of intensive diet and exercise on knee joint loads, inflammation, and clinical outcomes among overweight and obese adults with knee osteoarthritis. *Journal of the American Medical Association, 310*(12), 1263-1273.

MetLife Mature Market Institute. (2006*). The MetLife market survey of assisted living costs*. (Survey report). New York, NY: MetLife Mature Market Institute. Retrieved from the Investment News website: http://www.investmentnews.com/assets/docs/CI16665412.PDF

MetLife Mature Market Institute. 2012. *Market survey of long-term care costs*. New York, NY: MetLife Mature Market Institute. Retrieved from the MetLife website: https://www.metlife.com/assets/cao/mmi/publications/studies/2012/studies/mmi-2012-market-survey-long-term-care-costs.pdf

Mishel, L., Gould, E., Bivens, J. (2015). *Wage stagnation in 9 charts* (Research report). Washington, D.C.: Economic Policy Institute (EPI). Retrieved from the EPI website: http://s1.epi.org/files/2013/wage-stagnation-in-nine-charts.pdf

Mitchell, G., Polivka, L. & Wang, S. (2008). *Florida Program of All-Inclusive Care for the Elderly (PACE): A Preliminary Evaluation* (Report prepared for Florida Medicaid referenced in Moore, L. (2013). *Program of All-Inclusive Care for the Elderly [PACE]: Providing Integrated Community Care for the Frail Elderly*). Tallahassee, FL: Florida State University (FSU), Claude Pepper Center. Retrieved from the FSU website: http://coss.fsu.edu/subdomains/claudepeppercenter.fsu.edu_wp/wp-content/uploads/2015/04/PACE-updated.pdf

Molinari, V., Chiriboga, D., Branch, L., Cho, S., Turner, K., Guo, J., & Hyer, K. (2010). Provision of pharmacological services in nursing homes. *The Journals of Gerontology Series B, 65B*(1), 57-60.

Mollica, R., Kassner, E., Walker, L., & Houser, A. (2009). *Taking the long view: Investing in Medicaid home and community-based services is cost-effective* (Insight on the Issues Report no. 26). Washington, D.C.: AARP Public Policy Institute. Retrieved from the AARP website: http://assets.aarp.org/rgcenter/il/i26_hcbs.pdf

Mollica, R., Houser, A., & Ujvari, K. (2012). *Assisted living and residential care in the states in 2010* (Insight on the Issues Report no. 58). Washington, D.C.: AARP Public Policy Institute. Retrieved from the AARP website: http://www.aarp.org/content/dam/aarp/

research/public_policy_institute/ltc/2012/residential-care-insight-on-the-issues-july-2012-AARP-ppi-ltc.pdf

Molton, I. & Terrill, A. (2014). Overview of persistent pain in older adults. *American Psychologist, 69*(2), 197-207.

Moon, M. (2015). Improving Medicare financing: Are we up to the challenge? *Generations,* 39(2), 164-171.

Morath, E. (2010, August 23). Baby boomer bankruptcies on the rise. *Wall Street Journal* (Posted at Bankruptcy Blog). Retrieved from the Wall Street Journal website: http://blogs.wsj.com/bankruptcy/2010/08/23/baby-boomer-bankruptcies-on-the-rise/

Nadeau, Y. & Black, S. (2010). Mixed dementia: The most common cause of dementia? *The Canadian Journal of Diagnosis, 27*(4), 35-44.

National Alliance for Caregiving & AARP. (2009). *Caregiving in the U.S.* (Research Report). Bethesda, MD: National Alliance for Caregiving (NAC). Retrieved from the NAC website: http://www.caregiving.org/data/Caregiving_in_the_US_2009_full_report.pdf

National Alliance for Caregiving & National Center on Women and Aging at Brandeis University. (1999). *The Metlife juggling act study: Balancing caregiving with work and the costs involved.* Bethesda, MD: National Alliance for Caregiving (NAC). Retrieved from the NAC website: http://www.caregiving.org/data/jugglingstudy.pdf

National Association of Realtors. (2006). *Baby boomer survey shows big appetite for real Estate* (Press release). Chicago, IL: National Association of Realtors (NAR). NAR Press Release. Retrieved from the NAR website: http://archive.realtor.org/article/baby-boomer-survey-shows-big-appetite-real-estate

National Center for Assisted Living. (2015). *Advocacy: Medicaid and finance policy.* Washington, D.C.: National Center for Assisted

Living (NCAL). Retrieved from the NCAL website: http://www.ahcancal.org/ncal/advocacy/Pages/MedicaidFinance.aspx

National Center for Assisted Living. (n.d.). Resident profile. Washington, D.C.: National Center for Assisted Living (NCAL). Retrieved from the NCAL website: http://www.ahcancal.org/ncal/resources/Pages/ResidentProfile.aspx

National Committee for Quality Assurance. (2013). *Integrated care for people with Medicare and Medicaid: A roadmap for quality.* Washington, D.C.: National Committee for Quality Assurance (NCQA). Retrieved from the NCQA website: http://www.ncqa.org/portals/0/public%20policy/NCQAWhitePaper-IntegratedCareforPeoplewithMedicareandMedicaid.pdf

National PACE Association. (2015a). *What is PACE?* Alexandria, VA: National PACE Association (NPA). Retrieved from the NPA website: http://www.npaonline.org/website/article.asp?id=12&title=Who,_What_and_Where_Is_PACE?

National PACE Association. (2015b). *Who does PACE serve?* Alexandria, VA: National PACE Association (NPA) Retrieved from the NPA website: http://www.npaonline.org/website/article.asp?id=50&title=Who_Does_PACE_Serve?

National Registry of Evidence-based Programs. (2014). *Program of All-Inclusive Care for the Elderly (PACE)* (Evaluation report). Washington, D.C.: U.S. Department of Health and Human Services, Substance Abuse and Mental Health Services Administration (SAMHSA). Retrieved from the SAMHSA website: http://www.nrepp.samhsa.gov/ViewIntervention.aspx?id=316

Nepal, B., Brown, L., & Anstey, K. (2014). Rising midlife obesity will worsen future prevalence of dementia. *PLoS One, 9*(9).

Newcomer, R., Flores, C., & Hernandez, M. (2008). In S. Golant & J. Hyde (eds.) *The assisted living residence: A vision for the future* (pp. 351-378). Baltimore, MD: The Johns Hopkins University Press.

New York State Department of Health. (2013). *Guidelines for provision of personal care services in Medicaid managed care.* Albany, NY: New York State Department of Health (NYDOH). Retrieved from the NYDOH website: https://www.health.ny.gov/health_care/medicaid/redesign/docs/final_personal_care_guidelines.pdf

Ng, T. & Harrington, C. (2012). The data speak: A progress report on providing Medicaid HCBS for elders. *Generations, 36*(1), 14-20.

Ng, T., Harrington, C., Musumeci, M., & Reaves, E. (2014). *Medicaid home and community-based services programs: 2011 data update* (Report). Menlo Park, CA: Kaiser Family Foundation (KFF), Kaiser Commission on Medicaid and the Uninsured. Retrieved from the KFF website: http://kff.org/medicaid/report/medicaid-home-and-community-based-services-programs-2011-data-update/

Nicholson, J. (2013). Obesity: A mediator of inflammation complicating knee replacement. *Rheumatology Network.* Norwalk, CT: UBM Medica. Retrieved from the Rheumatology Network website: http://www.rheumatologynetwork.com/osteoarthritis/obesity-mediator-inflammation-complicating-knee-replacement

Nolan, D. (2012). Home is where the hearth is: New models for nursing homes (Issue brief). Sacramento, CA: California Health Care Foundation (CHCF). Retrieved from the CHCF website: http://www.chcf.org/~/media/MEDIA%20LIBRARY%20Files/PDF/PDF%20H/PDF%20HomeHearthNursingHomes.pdf

Office of the National Coordinator for Health Information Technology. (2013). *Health information technology in long-term and post-acute care.* Washington, D.C.: U.S. Department of Health and Human

Services, Office of the National Coordinator for Health Information Technology. Retrieved from the HealthIT.gov website: http://www. healthit.gov/sites/default/files/pdf/HIT_LTPAC_IssueBrief031513. pdf

Oregon Department of Human Services. (2010). *Memory Care Communities, Chapter 411, Division 17 of the Oregon Administrative Rules.* Salem, OR: Oregon Department of Human Services (DHS). Retrieved from the DHS website: https://www.dhs.state.or.us/policy/spd/rules/411_057.pdf

Ortiz, J. (2010). *Assisted living facilities* (Small Business Market Research Report). San Antonio, TX: Small Business Development Center Network (SBDCNET). Retrieved from the SBDCNET website: http://www.sbdcnet.org/small-business-research-reports/assisted-living-facilities

Ory, M., Hoffman R., Yee, J., Tennstedt, S., & Schulz, R. (1999). Prevalence and impact of caregiving: A detailed comparison between dementia and non-dementia caregiving. *The Gerontologist, 39*(2), 177-186.

Paraprofessional Healthcare Institute. (2005). *The role of training in improving the recruitment and retention of direct-care workers in long-term care* (Workforce Strategies no. 3). New York, NY: Paraprofessional Healthcare Institute (PHI). Retrieved from the PHI website: http://phinational.org/sites/phinational.org/files/clearinghouse/WorkforceStrategies3.pdf

Paraprofessional Healthcare Institute. (2009). *Providing personal care services to elders and people with disabilities: A model curriculum for direct-care workers.* New York, NY: Paraprofessional Healthcare Institute (PHI). Retrieved from the PHI website: http://phinational.org/workforce/resources/phi-curricula/personal-care-services-curriculum

Paraprofessional Healthcare Institute. (2014a). *Nurse aide training require-ments–2014.* New York, NY: Paraprofessional Healthcare Institute (PHI). Retrieved from the PHI website: http://phinational.org/sites/phinational.org/files/research-report/nurse-aide-training-require-ments-2014.pdf

Paraprofessional Healthcare Institute (PHI). (2014b). *Occupational projections for direct care workers* (PHI Fact Sheet). New York, NY: Paraprofessional Healthcare Institute (PHI). Retrieved from the PHI website: http://phinational.org/sites/phinational.org/files/phi-factsheet14update-12052014.pdf

Park-Lee, E., Sengupta, M., & Harris-Kojetin, L. (2013). Dementia special care units in residential care communities: United States, 2010 (Data brief, no. 134). Washington, D.C.: U.S. Department of Health and Human Services, Centers for Disease Control and Prevention (CDC), National Center for Health Statistics. Retrieved from the CDC website: http://www.cdc.gov/nchs/data/databriefs/db134.pdf

PBS Frontline (2013, July 30a). *Life and death in assisted living* (video). Arlington, VA: Public Broadcasting Services (PBS). Retrieved at the PBS website: http://www.pbs.org/wgbh/pages/frontline/life-and-death-in-assisted-living/

PBS Frontline (2013, July 30b). *Catherine Dawes: Assisted liv-ing is a "ticking time bomb"* (Video transcript). Arlington, VA: Public Broadcasting Services (PBS). Retrieved at the PBS website: http://www.pbs.org/wgbh/pages/front-line/social-issues/life-and-death-in-assisted-living/catherine-hawes-assisted-living-is-a-ticking-time-bomb/

Pew Charitable Trusts. (2013). *Retirement security across genera-tions* (Research report). Philadelphia, PA: Pew Charitable Trusts. Retrieved at the Pewtrusts website: http://www.

pewtrusts.org/~/media/legacy/uploadedfiles/pcs_assets/2013/ EMPRetirementv4051013finalFORWEBpdf.pdf

Pew Charitable Trusts. (2014). *A new financial reality: The balance sheets and economic mobility of Generation X* (Research report). Philadelphia, PA: Pew Charitable Trusts. Retrieved at the Pewtrusts website: http://www.pewtrusts.org/~/media/Assets/2014/09/Pew_ Generation_X_report.pdf

Pew Research Center. (2011). *The Generation gap and the 2012 elections* (Research report). Washington, D.C.: Pew Research Center. Retrieved at the Pew Research Center website: http://www.people-press.org/files/legacy-pdf/11-3-11%20Generations%20Release. pdf

Pew Research Center. (2014). *Attitudes about aging: A global perspective* (Research report). Washington, D.C.: Pew Research Center. Retrieved at the Pew Research Center website: http://www.pewglobal.org/files/2014/01/Pew-Research-Center-Global-Aging-Report-FINAL-January-30-20141.pdf .

Pew Research Center. (2015). *Comparing Millennials to other generations*. Washington, D.C.: Pew Research Center. Retrieved at the Pew Research Center website: http://www.pewsocialtrends. org/2015/03/19/comparing-millennials-to-other-generations/

Pezzin, L., Pollock, R., & Schone, B. (2008). Parental marital disruption, family type, and transfers to disabled elderly parents. *Journals of Gerontology Series B, 63*(6), S349-S358.

Pharr, J., Francis, C., Terry, C., &Clark, M. (2014). Culture, caregiving, and health: exploring the influence of culture on family caregiver experiences. *ISRN Public Health* (ejournal), 8 pages. Retrieved from http://dx.doi.org/10.1155/2014/689826

Phillips, C., Spry, K., Sloane, P., & Hawes, C. (2000). Use of physical restraints and psychotropic medications in Alzheimer special care units in nursing homes. *American Journal of Public Health*, *90*(1), 92-96.

Pioneer Network. (2015a). *Mission, Vision, Values*. Rochester, NY: Pioneer Network. Retrieved from the Pioneer Network website: https://www.pioneernetwork.net/AboutUs/Values/

Pioneer Network. (2015b). *About us*. Rochester, NY: Pioneer Network. Retrieved from the Pioneer Network website: https://www.pioneer-network.net/AboutUs/About/

Plassman, B., Langa, K., Fisher, G., Heeringa, S., Weir, D., Ofstedal, M. … Wallace, R. (2007). Prevalence of dementia in the United States: The Aging, Demographics, and Memory Study. *Neuroepidemiology*, *29*(1-2), 125-132.

Polson, D. (2011). *By our sides: The vital work of immigrant direct care workers* (Policy Brief #8). New York, NY: Direct Care Alliance. Retrieved at the Direct Care Alliance website: http://blog.directcarealliance.org/wp-content/uploads/2011/06/The-Vital-Work-of-Immigrant-Direct-Care-Workers_policybrief-8_.pdf

Prudential Life Insurance. (2014). *Financial experiences and behaviors among women* (Research Study). Newark, NJ: Prudential Life Insurance. Retrieved at the Prudential Life Insurance website: http://www.prudential.com/media/managed/wm/media/Pru_Women_Study_2014.pdf?src=Newsroom&pg=WomenStudy2014

Redfoot, D., Feinberg, L. & Houser, A. (2013). *The aging of the baby boom and the growing care gap: A look at future declines in the availability of family caregivers* (Insight on the Issues Report 85). Washington, D.C.: AARP Public Policy Institute. Retrieved from the AARP website: http://www.aarp.org/content/dam/aarp/research/public_policy_institute/ltc/2013/baby-boom-and-the-growing-care-gap-insight-AARP-ppi-ltc.pdf

Redfoot, D. & Houser, A. (2010). *More older people with disabilities living in the community: Trends from the National Long-Term Care Survey, 1984-2004* (Report no. 2010-08). Washington D.C.: AARP Public Policy Institute. Retrieved from the AARP website: http://assets. aarp.org/rgcenter/ppi/ltc/2010-08-disability.pdf

Reinhard, S., Given, B., Petlick, N., & Bemis, A. (2008). Supporting family caregivers in providing care. Chapter 14 in Hughes, R. (Ed.), *Patient safety and quality: An evidence-based handbook for nurses.* Rockville, MD.: U.S. Department of Health and Human Services, Agency for Healthcare Research and Quality. Retrieved from the National Institutes of Health website: http://www.ncbi.nlm.nih.gov/ books/NBK2665/

Reinhard, S., Levine, C., & Samis, S. (2012). *Home alone: Family caregivers providing complex chronic care* (Report prepared for the AARP Public Policy Institute and the United Healthcare Fund). Washington D.C.: AARP Public Policy Institute. Retrieved from the AARP website: http://www.aarp.org/home-family/caregiving/info-10-2012/home-alone-family-caregivers-providing-complex-chronic-care.html

Reinhard, S., Kassner, E., Houser, A., Ujvari, K., Mollica, R., & Hendrickson, L. (2014). *Raising expectations: A state scorecard on long-term services and supports for older adults, people with physical disabilities, and family caregivers, Second edition* (Research report prepared for AARP, The Commonwealth Fund, and the Scan Foundation). Washington D.C.: AARP Public Policy Institute. Retrieved from the AARP website: http://www.aarp.org/content/ dam/aarp/research/public_policy_institute/ltc/2014/raising-expectations-2014-AARP-ppi-ltc.pdf

Reynolds, S. & McIlvane, J. (2008). The impact of obesity and arthritis on active life expectancy in older Americans. *Obesity, 17*(2), 363-369.

Robert Wood Johnson Foundation. (2015a). *The Green House project*. Princeton, NJ: Robert Wood Johnson Foundation (RWJF). Retrieved from the RWJF website: http://www.rwjf.org/en/how-we-work/grants/grantees/the-green-house-project.html

Robert Wood Johnson Foundation. (2015b). *Cash and counseling* (Program Results Report). Princeton, NJ: Robert Wood Johnson Foundation (RWJF). Retrieved from the RWJF website: http://www.rwjf.org/content/dam/farm/reports/program_results_reports/2015/rwjf406468

Robert Wood Johnson Foundation. (2015c). *Cash and Counseling* (Evaluation report). Princeton, NJ: Robert Wood Johnson Foundation (RWJF). Retrieved from the RWJF website: http://www.rwjf.org/content/dam/farm/reports/program_results_reports/2015/rwjf406468

Robison, J. & Pillemer, K. (2007). Job satisfaction and intention to quit among nursing home staff: Do special care units make a difference? *Journal of Applied Gerontology, 26*(1), 95-112.

Rosch, P. (2013, December 16). *Stress, Alzheimer's and memory Loss*. Fort Worth, TX: American Institute of Stress (AIS). Retrieved from the AIS website: http://www.stress.org/stress-alzheimers-and-memory-loss/

Ruffing, V. & Bingham III, C. (2012). *Rheumatoid arthritis signs and symptoms*. Baltimore, MD: Johns Hopkins University, Arthritis Center. Retrieved from the Johns Hopkins Arthritis Center website. http://www.hopkinsarthritis.org/arthritis-info/rheumatoid-arthritis/ra-symptoms/

Sahyoun N., Pratt L, Lentzner H., Dey, A., & Robinson K. (2001). *The Changing Profile of Nursing Home Residents: 1985-1997* (Aging Trends: No.4.). Washington, D.C.: U.S. Department of Health and Human Services, Centers for Disease Control and Prevention

(CDC), National Center for Health Statistics. Retrieved from the CDC website: http://www.cdc.gov/nchs/data/ahcd/aging-trends/04nursin.pdf

Sands, L., Wang, Y., McCabe, G., Jennings, K., Eng, C., & Covinsky, K. (2006). Rates of acute care admissions for frail older people living with met versus unmet activity of daily living needs. *Journal of the American Geriatrics Society, 54*(2), 339-344.

Schmitt, R. (2015). Elder abuse: When caregiving goes wrong. Washington, D.C.: AARP. Retrieved from the AARP website: http://www.aarp.org/home-family/caregiving/info-2015/elder-abuse-assisted-living.html

Schore, J., Foster, L., & Phillips, B. (2006). Consumer enrollment and experiences in the cash and counseling program. *Health Services Research, 42*(1 Pt. 2), 446-466.

Schulz, R. & Sherwood, P. (2008). Physical and mental health effects of family caregiving. *American Journal of Nursing, 108* (9 Supplement), 23-27.

Seeman, T., Merkin, S., Crimmins, E., & Karlamangla, A. (2010). Disability trends among older Americans: National Health and Nutrition Examination Surveys, 1988-1994 and 1999-2004. *American Journal of Public Health, 100*(1), 100-107.

Semuels, A. (2015, April 21). Building better nursing homes. *The Atlantic.* Retrieved from The Atlantic website: http://www.theatlantic.com/business/archive/2015/04/a-better-nursing-home-exists/390936/

Shier, V., Khodyakov, D., Cohen, L., Zimmerman, S., & Saliba, D. (2014). What does the evidence really say about culture change in nursing homes? *The Gerontologist, 54* (Supplement 1), S6-S16.

Shiri, R., Karppinen, J., Leino-Arjas, P., Solovieva, S., & Vookari-Juntura, E. (2010). The association between obesity and low back pain: A meta-analysis. *American Journal of Epidemiology, 171*(2), 135-154.

Shub, D. & Kunik, M. (2009). Comorbidity: Psychiatric comorbidity in persons with dementia. *Psychiatric Times, 26*(4), 32-36.

Simmons, S., Durkin, D., Rahman, A., Choi, L., Beuscher, L., & Schnelle, J. (2012). Resident characteristics related to lack of morning care provision in long-term care. *The Gerontologist, 53*(1), 151-161.

Simon-Rusinowitz, L., Loughlin, D., & Mahoney, K. (2011). *How did cash and counseling participants spend their budgets, and why does that matter for CLASS?* (CLASS Technical Assistant Brief no. 8). Long Beach, CA: The Scan Foundation. Retrieved from the Scan Foundation website: http://www.thescanfoundation.org/sites/default/files/TSF_CLASS_TA_No_8_Spending_Cash_and_Counseling_FINAL.pdf

Smith, M., Davis, M., Stano, M., & Whedon, J. (2013). Aging baby boomers and the rising cost of chronic back pain: Secular trend analysis of longitudinal medical expenditures panel survey data for years 2000 to 2007. *Journal of Manipulative Physical Therapy, 36*(1), 2-11.

Sommers, A. (2009). Obesity among older Americans (Congressional Research Service Report no. 7-5700, RL34358). Washington, D.C.: U.S. Congress, Congressional Research Service (CRS). Retrieved from the CRS website: https://file.wikileaks.org/file/crs/RL34358.pdf

Sowers, M. & Karvonen-Gutierrez, C. (2010). The evolving role of obesity in knee osteoarthritis. *Current Opinion in Rheumatology, 22*(5), 533-537.

Span, P. (2015, June 8). Justice Department takes down barriers in retirement homes (Blog post). *New York Times.* Retrieved from New York Times website: http://www.nytimes.com/2015/06/09/health/

justice-department-takes-down-barriers-in-retirement-homes.
html?_r=0

Spencer, Beth. (2013). *Safety for people with dementia*. Ann Arbor, MI:
University of Michigan Geriatrics Center. Retrieved from the
University of Michigan website: http://www.med.umich.edu/1libr/
Geriatrics/SafetyAloneDementia.pdf

Spillman, B., Wolff, J., Freedman, V., & Kasper, J. (2014*). Informal
Caregiving for Older Americans: An Analysis of the 2011 National
Health and Aging Trends Study.* (Report prepared under contract #
HHSP23337003T between the Office of Disability, Aging and Long-
Term Care Policy [DALTCP] and the Urban Institute). Washington,
D.C.: U.S. Department of Health and Human Services, DALTCP.
Retrieved from the Office of the Assistant Secretary for Planning
and Evaluation website: http://aspe.hhs.gov/daltcp/reports/2014/
NHATS-IC.cfm#profile

Stone, R., Bryant, N., & Barbarotta, L. (2009). *Supporting culture change*
(Issue Brief). Washington, D.C.: The Commonwealth Fund (CF).
Retrieved from the CF website: http://www.commonwealthfund.
org/~/media/Files/Publications/Issue%20Brief/2009/Oct/1328_
Stone_supporting_culture_change_smarter_state_nursing_home_
reg.pdf

Stone, R. (2012). The long-term care workforce: From acciden-
tal to valued profession. In D. Wolf and N. Folbre (eds.),
*Universal coverage of long-term care in the United States: Can
we get there from here?* (pp. 155-178). Russell Sage Foundation
e-book, retrieved at https://www.russellsage.org/publications/
universal-coverage-long-term-care-united-states

Sullivan, E., Annest, J., Luo, F., Simon, T., & Dahlberg, L. (2013, May 3).
Suicide among adults aged 35-64 years – United States, 1999-2010
(Morbidity and Mortality Weekly Report). Washington, D.C.: U.S.

Department of Health and Human Services, Centers for Disease Control and Prevention (CDC). Retrieved from the CDC website: http://www.cdc.gov/mmwr/pdf/wk/mm6217.pdf

Temkin-Greener, H. & Mukamel, D. (2002). Predicting place of death in the Program of All-inclusive Care for the Elderly (PACE): Participant versus program characteristics. *Journal of the American Geriatrics Society, 50*(1), 125-135.

Tennstedt, S., Cafferata, G., & Sullivan, L. (1992). Depression among caregivers of impaired elderly. *Journal of Aging Health, 4*(1), 58-76.

Theis, K., Helmick, C., & Hootman, J. (2007). Report from the CDC: Arthritis burden and impact are greater among U.S. women than men: Intervention opportunities. *Journal of Women's Health, 19*(4). 441-453.

Tinetti, M. (2003). Preventing falls in elderly persons. *New England Journal of Medicine, 348*, 42-49.

Toossi, M. (2012). Labor force projections to 2020: A more slowly growing workforce. *Monthly Labor Review*. Washington, D.C.: U.S. Department of Labor, Bureau of Labor Statistics (BLS). Retrieved from the BLS website: http://www.bls.gov/opub/mlr/2012/01/art-3full.pdf

Torres, S. (2014). Aging women, living poorer. *Contexts, 13*(2). Retrieved from the Contexts website: http://contexts.org/articles/aging-women-living-poorer/

Trawinski, L. (2012). *Nightmare on Main Street: Older Americans and the mortgage market crisis* (Research report no. 2012-08). Washington, D.C.: AARP Public Policy Institute. Retrieved from the AARP website: http://www.aarp.org/content/dam/aarp/research/public_policy_institute/cons_prot/2012/nightmare-on-main-street-AARP-ppi-cons-prot.pdf

Vanderbilt Center for Quality Aging. (2013). *Quality of life: New strategy*. Nashville, TN: Vanderbilt University, Center for Quality Aging. Retrieved from the Vanderbilt University Center for Quality Aging website: http://www.mc.vanderbilt.edu/root/vumc.php?site=cqa&doc=43897

Vaartjes, I., O'Flaherty, M., Capewell, S., Kapelle, J., & Bots, M. (2013). Remarkable decline in ischemic stroke mortality is not matched by changes in incidence. *Stroke, 44,* 591-597.

Villarreal, P. (2012). *How are baby boomers spending their money?* (Policy report no. 341). Dallas, TX: National Center for Policy Analysis (NCPA). Retrieved from the NCPA website: http://www.ncpa.org/pub/st341

West, L., Cole, S., Goodkind, D., & He, W. (2014). *65+ in the United States: 2010* (Special report no. P23-212). Washington, D.C.: U.S. Department of Commerce, Census Bureau. Retrieved from the Census Bureau website: https://www.census.gov/content/dam/Census/library/publications/2014/demo/p23-212.pdf

Willgang, P. (2008). Medical direction and the future of assisted living. *Annals of Long-Term Care, 16*(3), 29-31.

Williams, J., Devaux, R., Petrac, P., & Feinberg, L. (2012*). Protecting family caregivers from employment discrimination.* (Insight on the Issues Report 68). Washington, D.C.: AARP Public Policy Institute. Retrieved from the AARP website: http://www.aarp.org/content/dam/aarp/research/public_policy_institute/health/protecting-care-givers-employment-discrimination-insight-AARP-ppi-ltc.pdf

Williams, W. & Wiener, J. (2015). The impact of assistive technologies on formal and informal home care. *The Gerontologist, 55*(3), 422-433.

Wilson, R., Capuano, A., Boyle, P., Hoganson, G., Hizel, L., Shah, R. ... Bennett, D. (2014) Clinical-pathologic study of depressive symptoms and cognitive decline in old age. *Neurology, 83*(8), 702-709.

Wunderlich, G. & Kohler, P., eds. (2001). Strengthening the Caregiving Work Force (Chapter Six). In *Improving the quality of long-term care.* Washington D.C.: Institute of Medicine, National Academies Press (NAP). Retrieved from the NAP website: http://www.nap.edu/openbook.php?record_id=9611

Wysocki, A., Kane, R., Golberstein, E., Dowd, B., Lum, T., & Shippee, T. (2014). The association between long-term care setting and potentially preventable hospitalizations among older dual eligibles." *Health Services Research. 49*(3), 778-797.

Xue, Q-L. (2011). The frailty syndrome: Definition and natural history. *Clinical Geriatric Medicine, 27*(1), 1-15.

Yang, Y. (2008). Social inequalities in happiness in the United States, 1972 to the present: An age-period-cohort analysis. *American Sociological Review, 73*(2), 204-226.

Yoder, S. (2012, January 26). The coming nursing home shortage. *The Fiscal Times.* Retrieved from the Fiscal Times website: http://www.thefiscaltimes.com/Articles/2012/01/26/The-Coming-Nursing-Home-Shortage

Zal, H. (1999). Agitation in the elderly. *Psychiatric Times (online), 16*(1). Retrieved from the Psychiatric Times website: http://www.psychiatrictimes.com/dementia/agitation-elderly

Zimmerman, S. & Cohen, L. (2010). Evidence behind the Green House and similar models of nursing home care. *Aging Health, 6*(6), 717-737.

About the author

Henry Moss is a retired baby boomer doing independent academic and public policy research and writing. He has a PhD in philosophy and has written on cognitive science and the history and philosophy of technological progress. His public policy interests include health care, housing and urban development, technological progress, and theories of social democracy. After teaching philosophy for several years, he was an educational administrator in private trade colleges. He can be contacted at hmoss011@gmail.com